D1590499

LOVE, LIES AND RUSSIAN SPIES

MIKE TERRY

ISBN 978-1-64468-134-3 (Paperback)
ISBN 978-1-64468-135-0 (Digital)

Copyright © 2020 Mike Terry
All rights reserved
First Edition

All rights reserved. No part of this publication may be reproduced, distributed, or transmitted in any form or by any means, including photocopying, recording, or other electronic or mechanical methods without the prior written permission of the publisher. For permission requests, solicit the publisher via the address below.

Covenant Books, Inc.
11661 Hwy 707
Murrells Inlet, SC 29576
www.covenantbooks.com

Dedication

To my precious wife Anna who tirelessly gave every ounce of herself to being my partner and to raising and homeschooling our children. She was always encouraging us to come out of our comfort zones and go for it. When I don't think I can go any farther. I can hear her saying, "Come on, Mike! Just a hundred more yards!"

CONTENTS

CHAPTER 1

⋙✦⋘

The Young and the Restless

*A*nna was the coolest and most laid-back girl that I had ever been around. We met through a friend in the summer of 1981 and had very similar interests, two of which were a love of the outdoors and smoking pot. We couldn't wait to spend time with each other every day.

We were both living back at home with our parents. I was working for a company that filed for bankruptcy, and I had just gotten my second DUI and lost my house and car. Anna had recently returned from the Ozarks where she was living off the land for a couple of years with her boyfriend. They built a cabin in the mountains with no electricity or running water, so their water came from a garden hose from a mountain spring. There wasn't a clean living to be made, except working part-time for the forest service building trails. Others grew pot, and some were busted and went to prison. We have hiked some of the trails many times that she helped build.

Anna broke up with her boyfriend after an argument and moved back to Memphis. She would pick me up in her old Honda Civic and drop me off at the golf course and go to her vet tech class. She would return to get me after school (I had it made), and we would usually get high and go to the park and throw the softball or hike some trails. She had the best arm of any girl that I had ever met (another reason I was so attracted to her). I was drawing unemployment, working part-time at a friend's liquor store, and selling pot and Quaaludes (disco biscuits as we used to call them).

We fell in love and decided to get married. I didn't want for us to live together because I had become a Christian in high school and didn't feel right about it. Also, first and foremost, I didn't want to hurt my mother. We went to marriage counseling and were told by the pastor that we needed to confront our spiritual differences because it would cause problems down the road. This was something that we hadn't talked about much, except me telling her that I was running from God and my heart's desire was to come back to Him, and she thought that was cool. We were married in 1982.

I want to take a little time to explain how and why we differed on this major issue. My senior year in high school, I was hoping to go to Ole Miss on a baseball scholarship or get drafted and go straight to the pros. The summer before my senior year between playing baseball and working out for football, my friends and I would go camping and do LSD. It was fun but didn't have a positive effect on my pitching. (One night I tried to pick somebody off first base who wasn't there.)

One Saturday afternoon that summer, I walked across the street to my hippie neighbor's house and asked him, "Do you have any pot for sale?"

He said, "No, I became a Christian, and I'm not doing dope anymore. Will you go to church with me tomorrow?"

I responded, "I will sometime, but I can't tomorrow."

He called me every Saturday and asked me if I wanted to go, and near the end of summer, I decided to go with him because football season was about to start. We were pre-ranked number 1 in the state, and I assumed that if I went to church, God would bless my efforts. We went to church, and I saw some of my old hippie friends worshiping God. I had never seen anybody truly worship before because I had grown up in a very traditional (dead) denomination.

My friend's church was a charismatic church in Whitehaven that was reaching out to the wild and crazy longhaired kids of that era, and they invited everyone to come "just as you are." During the service, I sensed God telling me that I needed Him. I prayed and simply told God, "I need You!" For the first time I really felt the Holy Spirit's presence.

From that point on, I began to see Christian bumper stickers and started running into people that wanted to tell me about Jesus and was flooded with other types of mysterious signs of this nature. I tried to make myself believe that it was all coincidence, but it happened so often that I knew God was chasing me. I decided that I wanted to become a Christian but didn't think I could give up the drugs or the sexual relationship I was having with my girlfriend. I just decided and believed that I was going to hell.

Finally, I thought I could give up everything but the pot. Football season had started, and we were undefeated and playing the next to the last game of the season and were behind eight to seven, fourth down on their five-yard line with just a few seconds left. Back then high school kickers didn't attempt many field goals, and I was the kicker and hadn't missed any extra points all year. I told my coach to let me kick it, and I felt very confident. Then right before the snap, I told God, "Let me miss this if the pot is a sin." Guess what? Yep, wide to the left! I still get ribbed about that even from players from the opposing team.

I still wanted to quit my crazy lifestyle but couldn't. After football season, I was going to a school dance and when I was getting ready, I turned on the TV and Billy Graham was preaching. I sat down and listened, and he described the lifestyle I was living and talked about the moving away of folks from God in the end times. When I stepped into the shower, I felt like I could give my life to Christ, and I cried out to Jesus, "Take my life." I felt a rush like I had never experienced before and was overwhelmed with peace and joy.

I was so thrilled to go to the dance and tell all my friends what had happened, but they weren't too excited and unfortunately a week later I was back doing the drugs. The next weekend I called a buddy and asked him, "Do you want to get high and go to the basketball game with me?"

He said, "I'll go to the game with you but a couple of nights ago I flipped out on acid and went to my preacher's house and gave my life back to God."

I was so excited because I was needing some help and support. We stopped at a gas station on the way, and I gave my dope to a friend (I thought it would have been a shame to throw all that good weed away), and I told him what had happened. I noticed a shocked but very pleased expression on his face when he checked out the surprise he had received.

We went to the game and someone tapped me on the shoulder and asked me, "Can I share something with you?" It was a pamphlet explaining the Gospel, and for the first time I really understood it. Jesus died on the cross as punishment for my sins. He was buried and God raised Him from the dead on the third day, and if I believed this and gave my life to Christ, I would have eternal life. It turns out the guy was an All American baseball player at Ole Miss and was one of my heroes. The next day we invited two carloads of our friends to his place, and they all became Christians, and most are still involved in some type of ministry to this day.

Unfortunately, soon after, I began having serious, bizarre doubts about the Bible and my faith. I couldn't stop trying to figure it out. (Fifteen years later, I discovered that this was an obsessive-compulsive thought disorder which progressed more and more.) Sleep was the only relief I experienced, but many nights I would wake up with my mind racing and be back in the unending battle.

After graduating from high school in 1973, I didn't go to Ole Miss but attended Jackson State on a baseball scholarship for two years and then on to a redshirt year at Memphis State. I was giving my testimony at many churches and events throughout my senior year in high school and freshman year in college, even though I was still going through mental torment. I could barely stay in touch with reality and communicate. I can remember standing on the pitcher's mound and arguing inside my head about whether I had committed the unpardonable sin. For almost two years, I still couldn't get the horrible thoughts out of my head and felt hopeless for relief.

By the start of my sophomore year in college, I couldn't stand it any longer, so I started to have a few beers to sedate myself. The church I was attending believed it was a sin to have anything to drink, so I began to think I was out of fellowship with God and couldn't pray, except for Him to help me repent and bring me back. I prayed this prayer every night, but very soon I was back into serious drugs. The only good thing that came out of it was I started to relax and pitch and hit the baseball better than I ever had. God didn't reward it because I had a couple of injuries that hindered my performance, and I didn't get drafted which I always assumed I would.

The few years after college before I met Anna, I got more deeply involved in drugs. I would drink a fifth of whiskey on the rocks before heading out in my car to bars to pick up women (real smart). I thought nothing of it until a couple of DUIs and a crash that almost ended my life, and this was my state of mind and lifestyle when I met Anna. We were married right after she finished school, and she went to work for a veterinarian. She always had a love for animals and had a pet squirrel, a cat, and a wonderful golden retriever. She loved adventure and was always ready to try something new. I went to work for Memphis Light Gas and Water as an industrial coatings specialist (a glorified painter).

We started to save some money and decided that we could afford some cocaine (financial geniuses). Both of our focal points were looking forward to getting high, and I really enjoyed the cocaine and was drinking a lot of whiskeys. That combination made me very uninhibited and Anna made me give up the whiskey forever. I found my life spiraling more and more out of control and was buying cocaine and doing half of it with Anna and a half before I got home.

My boss at work was treating us unfairly making us carry fifty-pound bags of sand up a twelve-foot step ladder to dump into a sandblaster, where the proper way was to put about ten pounds in a five-gallon bucket. One of my coworkers weighed about one hundred twenty pounds, and this was very dangerous for him, and I found myself building up a lot of hatred in my heart for the boss and was foolishly considering have someone do him harm (he was a lot bigger than me). Every night when I climbed in my bed I would pray the prayer I mentioned earlier and ask God to deliver me from the drugs and hatred because I was surely spiraling out of control and especially regretted lying to Anna about her share of the coke.

One day at work while I was waiting for tools at the equipment desk, I became overwhelmed with the thought that I could surrender everything back to God. I told Him to take control of my life like I did in the shower in high school, and at once I felt the addictions and hatred lift (the Holy Spirit is very real). Then the reality set in that I was going to go home and tell Anna what had happened to me. She took the news fairly well, and for several months, she would be on one end of the sofa with the bong and me on the other end reading the Bible. This drastic change in my lifestyle was especially difficult for her. She didn't complain, but I knew it was tough, and she continued to go out and have fun with her friends on the weekends, and I trusted her totally.

CHAPTER 2

⊰✕⊱

Going down to the River

I had started to go to church again at Bellevue Baptist, and I just knew if I could get Anna to go hear Adrian Rogers preach that she would come to Christ. She had grown up in a very loving family but agnostic at best about the things of God. She finally went with me on a Wednesday night and to my disappointment, it was a meeting about finances and long term planning. She said she had figured the place was probably just all about money, and I realized right then that it was up to the Holy Spirit to bring her to Christ and not a church or any preacher.

I continued to attend, and she would go with me every once in a while, and there were many people praying for her including my mom and dad. They would give an invitation every Sunday for people to come forward for spiritual needs, and one Sunday she looked at me and asked me if I would go with her. I was so shocked, it took me a minute to get out of my seat and catch up with her. The message was about God's original intent for man to live with him in a perfect world, but man decided to do it his way and walked away from God, and that God has a plan to reconcile us to Himself through Jesus through the perfect life He lived for us. She believed at that moment, giving her life to Christ and surrendered everything to him instantly and was baptized that night.

For Anna, unlike having the addictive personality that I did, she could always take the drugs or leave them and never had a problem with alcohol (probably from watching me act a fool). For her, this was the purpose in life and adventure she had been yearning for. Now she could interact daily with the God of the universe, and we were so excited, to say the least. She was twenty-four at the time and I was twenty-eight, and we immediately got involved together in that awesome church and met some wonderful people. For the next five years, we participated in discipleship training programs and began to lead small groups of Christians with which we could get to know and share life together.

I still fought the obsessive thoughts every day but learned to manage them by learning to *recognize* the crazy thoughts, *refuse* to reason with them, and then *replace* them with the truth. I learned that it was spiritual warfare, and that there were real spirits opposed to what I believed (more about encountering these spirits in different forms in a foreign land later). I struggled but was able to keep it from interfering too much with my daily life by using this technique. After five years we decided to have kids and our first child was born in 1988, Natalie, a beautiful, precious little girl. Three years later we had a son, Reid, who is still the coolest guy I know. We made up our minds that we were going to spend time with the kids, not just quality time, and I had a wonderful example to follow. My parents never missed a ball game, even in college, if it was within a day's driving distance of Memphis. One time we were playing in Jackson, Tennessee, and my dad told me he didn't think he could get off work, but at game time, I looked out in the parking lot, and he pulled up one of those old yellow Memphis Light Gas and Water trucks. There was never a doubt in my mind about whether they loved me, and we wanted Natalie and Reid to have the same assurance.

After working at MLG&W for five years, in 1986, I left my job with the city and started a paint contracting business (a glorified painter with crew). Anna left the vet tech position and joined the business hanging wallpaper, and we had some prominent wealthy clients from Bellevue church and started to make a nice living. It was in the eighties during the wallpaper heyday and Anna was especially raking it in. She worked until she was nine months pregnant with

Natalie and then was able to fulfill her goal of being a stay at home mom and hung paper on the side.

We had six acres in Fayette County and were able to raise our kids in the country, and they are both grateful for the experience. When it came time for the kids to go to school, we made a decision to homeschool because the public schools in our area were the worst academically in the state and had safety issues. I am amazed at Anna's dedication and the sacrifice she made to put her career on hold and stay home and teach the kids.

We were going to a small community church with plenty of activities for the children. Anna and I were both leaders in the church, and things seemed to be going smoothly in all areas of our lives, and we appeared to have the model marriage. We spent time praying together as a family and were able to reach out to neighbors as needs arose.

About the time Natalie became a teenager, she and Anna started butting heads. It was nothing major but just the normal mother-daughter relationship for that season of life. We decided to move back into Shelby county for Natalie to go to high school, and Reid continued to homeschool until high school age.

We began attending Life Link church in Lakeland. It was a wonderful church, but one of the drawbacks was that there weren't many teenagers for Natalie to hang out with, although there were plenty of boys Reid's age and a dedicated leader. After a few years, I became ordained as a minister, and my responsibility became pastoring the people by leading home groups, counseling, and visiting and praying for the sick. Anna's heart quickly turned toward foreign missions, and she soon became very passionate about it, to say the least.

It was September 2001 and the terrorist attack of that year caused great fear in many areas of people's lives, one being their finances. I noticed quickly that some of my main contractors were slowing down because their clients were afraid to spend money. It became obvious that I needed to do something else, and I started back to school to finish a pastoral counseling degree in hopes of getting paid a salary at a church. I went for a year and just ended up taking the counseling courses (I still wouldn't be finished if I tried to get the degree), and I also wanted to find out what the heck was wrong with my head. I had the compulsive thoughts somewhat under control by using the technique I described earlier, but it was still a difficult day to day struggle.

For our final exam, we counseled each other, and after listening to my story about my mind battles, the pastor who was counselling me told me that he thought I had a chemical imbalance and needed medicine. The next day I went to my general practitioner and told him what was happening. He prescribed Zoloft, and two days later, I was able to regain control of my thoughts. I found out that this can be a trial and error process, but the Zoloft worked for me. If you are in trouble mentally and feel like there is no hope, I guarantee you that there is!

In my search for a new career, I went to the library (folks still did that in those days.) and got a copy of Entrepreneur Magazine's annual Franchise 500 issue. I prayed and asked God to show me something that I could do, and I noticed Visiting Angels Senior Homecare. It jumped out at me because Anna and I had been taking care of my dad for the past two years after suffering a stroke. He was totally paralyzed on the left side and was incontinent, and I never knew any care or daily help like that existed. We decided that it was a good fit and sold our Coca-Cola stock and invested all the money we could borrow and bought the franchise in February of 2002.

Neither of us had experienced the level of stress that was ahead of us in the first few years of business. It was 24-7, but we still participated in our kids' sports and other activities and tried to be involved in ministry. I can remember coaching Reid's baseball games and Anna sitting in the stands with her list of caregivers trying to schedule emergency cases.

After the first year, we had ten clients and about twenty CNAs. It was basically Anna and I running the business in the beginning, and it was nuts because we had some clients with difficult needs. During the next couple of years, our clients increased, but we got behind with payroll taxes and owed the IRS about $150,000. During year four it was too much pressure for Anna, still homeschooling Reid, and she backed out of the business. I hired a couple of dependable office workers, but they still couldn't answer phones after hours and make a decision without calling me.

I had a heart attack in year five, and my cardiologist told me that the business was killing me at the ripe old age of fifty-three. Later that year I finally decided to start making major adjustments in billing, hiring, and correcting cash flow issues. These were things that the franchise had taught us to do, but I thought I knew best (hard headed) and didn't follow their advice.

Reid started high school, and Anna took a job working in a frame shop, mainly because our health insurance cost had gone through the roof. She was a wonderful artist and put much of that on hold, and the frame shop was right for her. After a year because she was in a group plan, we were able to start a group plan with Visiting Angels (still don't understand how all that worked).

The business was still teetering, and I found some creative ways to make payroll (not illegal, but too borderline to write in this book). I went to Houston to meet with the owner of the franchise, a wonderful guy who truly cared for us. My goal was to see if he would take back the franchise. He told me about a couple of drastic things to do and said to pray and ask God that if He wanted us to stay in the business to make it turn around in three months. He said, if not, he would buy back the business, so I agreed to the challenge and headed back to Memphis.

The sales doubled over the next few months, and we actually started to make a profit, which totally blew us away. We were able to hire two highly skilled case managers who would alternate with our office manager and be on call after hours. This freed me up to concentrate on growing the business and have more time for church ministry. Also, this allowed Anna to reenter the business and do what she enjoyed most, which was visiting and spending quality time with our precious senior clients. She would also take sales calls because she was beyond a doubt the best homecare salesperson I had ever met. Our sixth-year sales went from $600,000 annually to over a million.

CHAPTER 3

※※※

Finally Got a Piece of the Pie

*A*nna began to develop a huge heart for overseas missions and helping the poorest of the poor in third world countries. That year she visited countries in Central America and worked with medical teams and taught art to children. She was also able to work for a mission agency from home and send donations, supplies, and missionaries all over the world.

We had the business running pretty much on its own, which was my intent. I was able to take off one day a week and take some more counseling courses, which I did for about a year. I became certified in marriage, drug and alcohol abuse, and PTSD. I am mentioning all this not to toot our horn with a list of accomplishments but to help describe the platform from which we were able to set out on our next to last mind-blowing adventure (stuff you can't make up).

In the seventh year, 2009, we grossed $2,000,000, had ninety caregivers and about eighty monthly clients. We started to make a lot of money, and Anna began to be more and more involved with missions. We were supporting missionaries, and she made two different month-long trips to India. One was ministering to young girls that had been rescued from sex trafficking and spending time with girls whose mothers were prostitutes. Their mothers would drop them off soon after birth on the front doorstep of, Joel, our Indian pastor friend's orphanage, so they wouldn't have to be brought up in that lifestyle and they would have hope for the future. We were able to provide school uniforms and mattresses for about thirty of them. The next year she went to a remote village in the mountains in India with no running water. The women spent most of their time hauling water from a stream in a valley below. Anna and her team built a well and solved that major time-consuming, backbreaking problem.

When Anna came back, she was convinced that I should join her endeavors. Natalie and Reid even went with her to work in a village in Central America. I hadn't had a real two-week vacation since we started the business and told her, "If I take time off I'm gonna sit my butt on a beach somewhere or on the porch of a mountain cabin." We celebrated our twenty-fifth wedding anniversary that summer and spent a wonderful ten days in Italy together. We went on a couple more relaxing trips like that, and I finally told Anna that I would be willing to go on a mission trip.

I didn't have a clue what role I could play and soon found out from a missionary friend in Nicaragua that the boys and men there played baseball every day, except during the rainy season, so he suggested I do a baseball camp. Many of their mothers took a bus to the capital and worked as prostitutes and lived in huts, some without doors. Interestingly enough, most had a TV with communist propaganda stations pumped in.

I called a buddy that I had played ball with in college and asked him, "Do you want to go on a mission trip with me and organize a baseball camp?"

He said without hesitating, "Yeah I sure would. When do we leave?"

He was coaching at a high school in Memphis and had recently won the national championship and had been named USA Today's national coach of the year. We were both very excited and did this the next two summers and started out working with boys. Men from neighboring villages were watching us, and we began going from one village to another also instructing them. Most of the little towns had a baseball park. Some were also cow pastures and one time a cow stopped on first base and urinated, to nobody's surprise. My partner taught them so much and I just assisted. The method of teaching fundamentals had improved tenfold, and I hadn't kept up with it. At the end of each practice, with the help of a translator, I would talk to them about how to win the game of life, and many had never heard this message of Christ.

Soon after the second trip, Anna and I visited my cousin in Dallas, and right before we headed back to Memphis, we attended his church. The message was about how we all are called to GO. This could be going across the street to help a neighbor in need or going across the world to minister to the poor. I began feeling like God wanted me to give my life to missions at home and abroad. While we were waiting to get on the plane, a group of about twenty people were returning from a mission trip. On the back of their T-shirts was a stoplight with the green light highlighted and the letters GO in bold bright green. I had chill bumps and knew that was my calling, and Anna was thrilled because we were on the same page with missions and could continue on this adventure together.

At the beginning of that year, before I went to Nicaragua, Anna and others from our church were volunteering with Catholic Charities in Memphis. The Memphis center was a major stop for large groups of refugees entering our country. Anna and some friends were teaching ESL classes and helping them assimilate into our culture by hanging out with them and helping them find employment.

Anna came home one day and told me that she had met a really cool and smart fellow, Arman, who had just arrived by political asylum from Uzbekistan. She said he began teaching ESL classes because he already spoke fluent English. She said he had been a prosperous businessman and couldn't contact his former clients because he fled the country. She wanted to know if I could meet him and introduce him to some of my contacts. I believed that would be a wonderful idea and agreed to get together to determine what kind of business he would be interested in.

Arman and I spent an afternoon together getting to get to know each other at a folk art festival downtown while Anna enjoyed the exhibits. He was very interesting and spoke better English than I did (bigger vocabulary anyway). Come to find out his daughter and nephews had been exchange students in Mississippi. He had been here many times and had helped a Mississippi university start modern cotton farming in Uzbekistan. He claimed to have lost everything and wanted to know if I had been involved in international business. I informed him that we helped some folks start a cattle business in Central America, and because of it, they were able to support themselves, and I enjoyed the process and believed it was maybe the best way to help the poor. He said he had some ideas about doing international business that could fund many projects like this. He wasn't able go back to Central Asia or Russia but was looking for someone who might be able to get in touch with his partners and finish some lucrative deals that were in the works. One venture was selling used cotton equipment from America in Kazakhstan to hopefully accomplish there what they did in Uzbekistan, and I was very intrigued, to say the least. He had other ideas that blew me away that I thought would fit right in with our mission activities. Lights started going off in my head about how this might be God's way of making a lot of money to give to causes we believed in.

Arman said one of his contacts from Kazakhstan, Erkin, was coming here to visit and wondered if I would meet with him. He was working in the cotton business and was meeting with some brokers in Arkansas. Arman didn't have a car, so I picked up Erkin at the airport. He didn't speak any English but appeared to be a seasoned businessman with money. Before he went back home, he suggested I come to visit him and find out what they were doing, and maybe we could start some joint ventures.

I told him I was a Christian and asked him and Arman if they wanted to go to church with us before I took him back to the airport. Erkin had told me earlier that he wasn't a Christian but believed in spirits and needed prayer. He seemed to be obsessed with taking pictures. He took a picture of the worship team when they were singing and showed me the picture and there were bright colorful images over their heads. He said that the images were angels. This phenomenon happened at sunset on the Mississippi River and several other places. Other pictures didn't have the images. We prayed for him at the end of the service. He had never been to an evangelical church and I found out later that Christians in Kazakhstan are harassed and closely monitored by the government. Arman began going to church with us most Sundays for the next few years and really seemed to enjoy it and get a lot out of it (never made a commitment to Christ as far as I know).

Anna and I decided that my going to Kazakhstan would be an exciting doorway for missions, and we agreed that it would be a good idea for me to go and explore the opportunities. We had meetings with Arman discussing different business and mission options, and Arman and I soon formed an LLC. Natalie came on board after school each day and helped build a website and assisted us in putting a business plan on paper, and we came up with many ideas. The cotton business, cultural exchange (sports in the beginning), starting a senior homecare business, and bringing young entrepreneurs to Memphis for ESL classes and business training was just the beginning.

Our homecare business was running on its own, which had been my goal, and we were making a nice profit (greater than we had ever imagined). Besides supporting missionaries around the world, we had enough to finance our own trips without asking for donations, and our plans for the next trip were full steam ahead. We decided it would also be a timely life experience for Natalie, and she went along as my administrative assistant and scheduled all of our appointments and was a valuable asset.

As we were making plans, Arman suggested we also go to Moscow. He had contacts in Russia and believed that part of the world to be ready for the homecare business, and I spoke to the owners of my franchise about it. They had begun to go international and authorized me to set up a master franchise in Russia. We met with local and state officials in Memphis and set up meetings with trade officials in Kazakhstan and in Moscow. During those days our government was trying to improve relations with Russia, and we assumed we had their blessing and approval.

The pre-arranged meetings were to begin with Erkin's contacts in Almaty, Kazakhstan for a couple days and establish an office with him for joint ventures. Then we would meet Arman's contacts in sports and then others that might have an interest in business training. We were to spend seven days in Almaty and then head to

Moscow to spend another seven days meeting with those interested in homecare and also prospects for the business training classes.

One thing Arman told us that we needed to be aware of was that every business meeting in that part of the world was preceded by a vodka toast. I hated the taste of vodka. I didn't have a problem with a toast as far as my beliefs were concerned as I had come to believe that Jesus didn't turn the water into grape juice (as I was taught earlier) and that the warnings in scripture were about getting drunk. We didn't force teetotaling on Natalie and Reid. After being set free from my problem with whiskey, I had decided not to drink it anymore. Arman decided we have a vodka toast as practice, so Natalie and I tossed one down and tried not to show an expression.

The Sunday before we set out for Almaty, Anna and I gave a slide presentation about our mission trips at church. At the end of the service, a tall, jovial, elderly gentleman, Jimmy, approached me with a friendly smile on his face. He said enthusiastically, "I heard you mention that you were going to Kazakhstan and Moscow. I've been there before on business and am looking for mazut, which is a heating oil produced in the former Soviet Union. I have a client in China looking for this commodity. Can you keep an eye open for it while you are there?"

I was glad to tell him, "Sure, just email me the specs and a proposal!"

CHAPTER 4

><🕸<

Leavin' on a Jet Plane

*I*t was January 2010, and Natalie and I were off to Almaty with a connecting flight through Raleigh, North Carolina, and then to Frankfurt, Germany. I had been through the Frankfurt airport before and struggled a bit, but this time Natalie guided me through the maze to our final seven-hour connection to Almaty, after a three-hour layover. I discovered the excellent customer service on Asian flights when they were very attentive to our needs and really seemed to enjoy their jobs. After about an hour, one of the flight attendants noticed Natalie dozing and suggested she stretch out across an unoccupied center isle of the airbus. She gave Natalie a couple of pillows and a blanket, and she slept like a baby for the rest of the trip. I can't sleep on an airplane. They offered me a large free glass of wine, and I still was unable to sleep.

As we were approaching the airport, I looked down and saw airplanes parked everywhere and not any order to it. I didn't see a runway but lights marking one and everything was covered with snow. I thought, "Yep, we are going to land right on the snow." When we landed they rolled out portable steps and we walked across the snow into the terminal which consisted of three waiting areas.

It was about 2:00 a.m. their time, and they were exactly twelve hours ahead of Memphis. Going through customs was fairly smooth, and the daughter of one of our contacts, Amina, took us to a nice Holiday Inn in Almaty. She was the hotel manager, and by the time we were settled in our room, it was about 4:00 a.m. We got a little sleep and went down and had a nice breakfast (had some food there that I recognized). Looking out the window, we noticed the breath-taking snow-covered mountains surrounding Almaty and crystal clear blue skies.

Our first meeting was scheduled at 9:00 a.m. A young friend of Erkin, who also served as our translator, picked us up at about ten thirty (we found out that Kazakhs are usually late). We met Erkin at a nice café called Noodles at the Kazakhstan Hotel, which turned out to be a great place to meet businessmen from all over the world, and I dined and hung out there often, while in Almaty, for the next few years.

Next, he took us to his office where we were warmly welcomed by his business associates over vodka toasts (and a tray of horse meat which Arman hadn't warned us about). They said all kinds of won-derful things about us and our future hopeful business relationships and close friendships that would last for a lifetime. We met at least fifteen of his partners in various businesses. Two were in the cotton business, several involved in fuel transportation, and some in other occupations. There was an interesting couple that dealt in ancient Chinese and Hebrew relics and an owner of a gold mine.

We had a ribbon cutting celebrating the opening of our joint venture office and had individual discussions with each group about possibilities. I decided to ask Erkin about the mazut that Jimmy had mentioned, and he said that was no problem and that he would work on a quote. He handed me a flash drive of the relics to bring back home to see if I could find some interest. He said they were interested in modern American trucking and the GPS technology, so I men-tioned that I had friends in the business and would find out if any of them would want to do some consulting on the subject. Another venture they truly desired was setting up a FedEx hub in their coun-try (more about this important issue later). They were attempting to rebuild the ancient Silk Road, which made its way through the area in centuries past.

That night, they took us out to eat, and then Natalie and I went back to the hotel and crashed for about ten hours. Erkin picked us up the next morning and took us on a drive up into the mountains surrounding Almaty, which is one of the most beautiful and tallest mountain ranges in the world. Afterward, they had a traditional Kazakh feast for us with a table setting fit for royalty (some horse meat, horse and camel milk along with traditional American food). We found out that horse meat and milk were a regular part of their diet. They had a slightly creamy soup which was a mixture of camel milk and horse meat broth (they said it was for health). Natalie was very uncomfortable with the horse meat because of her love for horses, but said the broth wasn't terrible (both were nasty tasting to me). They donned us in traditional Kazakh outfits. Our hostess claimed to be a numerologist for the president, and she asked us for our birthdays and started telling us facts about ourselves. I quickly changed the subject and told her we were Christians and also received supernatural guidance (that conversation ended). Amina was with us and was a former psychic at the Kremlin and advised the Soviet military (didn't realize that position existed). The third morning we had a business meeting with Erkin and decided on plans to move forward in the near future with Arman following up with them from Memphis on Skype.

After lunch, we met with a friend of Arman's, Vlad, who was a boxing coach for many of the Russian Olympic and professional champions, and he took us to a school where young potential athletes spend their early lives. They trained gymnasts, weight lifters, track and field participants, boxers and many other types of athletes. We met two former Olympic boxing champions who were instructors at the school and met with the director and discussed ways for potential sporting event exchanges between our countries in the future. He was very interested in our advanced weight training systems because, surprisingly, all they had available were the traditional free weights.

Vlad took us to meet two professional boxers at the school who were training for a fight and were both Olympic gold medalists. Their manager was with them, and I told him it would be wonderful if we could arrange some pro fights in Almaty and in Memphis, and he interpreted that to mean that I was certain I could make it happen (uh-oh). They were on their way shortly to a press conference which was going to be on TV and asked Natalie and me to attend. During the conference, to Natalie's and my utter surprise, they asked us to come sit at a table with the boxers under bright lights and cameras. They told the audience that we were from Memphis and were going to arrange some fights both in Memphis and in Almaty. Through a translator, I told the audience that I thought it would be wonderful for our countries, and my hopes were to make it happen (insert both feet in mouth).

Afterward, Vlad and his wife and his very intelligent, sweet fifteen-year-old daughter, who served as our translator, took us sightseeing in the city (Google "Almaty"—really beautiful). and then out to eat. We had mentioned to Vlad about the proposal we had for Mazut, and he had a friend, Alamut, who was in the commodity business and would also be able to prepare a quote. Alamut would become a contact for us on future visits for selling Angus beef in local markets and to the Kazakhstan military through his father, who was a high ranking official in their country's ministry of defense.

First thing the next morning we went to the American Embassy and met with officials who were overseeing American business projects. They were very cooperative and proved to be good assets over the next few years, and they would also be aware of our presence in Almaty in case any trouble arose.

That afternoon we met our next contact, Peter, who was involved in the hospitality business. He was looking for investors to build a very private upscale resort at Cosmodrome which is the world's first and largest space launch facility. Tourists would be able to see rockets launched from a partially underground and protected theatre, and other attractions would resemble our Epcot Center and showcase their advanced space technology. The Cosmodrome located in southern Kazakhstan, not too far from Almaty, wasn't like our launching sites in that the press wasn't welcome or allowed except on special occasions. A local told us this amphitheater would be an especially interesting place to observe the launches because of the absence of news media. He said they didn't have to be as concerned for the safety of their cosmonauts as us and were more experimental (WOW).

Peter had other ideas for business, and his wife took Natalie shopping and to a popular ski resort which was preparing for the Asian Winter Olympics. It was also the home of the world's highest outdoor skating rink perched near the top of one of the peaks. Afterward, we showed them a PowerPoint presentation that Natalie had prepared about our business training program, but being in the hospitality business, he was more interested in organizing some type of tourist exchange. We felt like it had been a very successful visit to Almaty, and we left there with certainty that we were going to put legs on the plans we discussed. I returned three more times for more extended stays exploring other deals and making connections.

We were off to Moscow and Arman's friends Marta and Maria, who were sisters, picked us up at the airport. The snow was cleared off the runway and the airport was much more sophisticated when we arrived about 9:00 p.m. after about a seven-hour flight. We went straight to a sports restaurant and bar which appeared to be a medieval castle. And low and behold when we walked in, Russia was playing the USA in hockey, and I sort of feared for our safety and hoped they wouldn't notice us, but they were a very friendly bunch. Maria's husband was there and was a husky, rather stoic City of Moscow policeman. When we finished dinner they took us to a very old, but nice, high rise apartment building which was similar to much of the housing in Moscow, located near a subway station.

Marta and Maria were Russian Orthodox and attended mass regularly. Marta was in the gold leaf business (real gold) when the former Soviet Union fell. She felt like they were in the right place at the right time since they were the first in this trade to begin restoring the old Russian cathedrals. A cathedral inside the Kremlin walls, which we visited, was their showcase. She came to Memphis about a year later and there was no market for this style of decor, as we were informed by several high-end decorators. Marta's sister was very interested in getting into the homecare business and that was our first order of business. We had an appointment at the American Embassy the first thing the next morning because we wanted to discuss the legality of starting an American franchise in Russia and also let them know we were there for our own safety precautions.

There were no American assisted living businesses in Russia at the time, and we discovered while in Almaty that everyone had always cared for their own seniors in the former Soviet Union. Kazakhstan wasn't even open to the possibility of hiring someone for that purpose but Moscow had more of a need and was gradually changing. Wealthy people who traveled for business were bringing in caregivers from Ukraine and the hiring process was done much differently. The lady we spoke with at the embassy put us in touch with an American law firm that could answer our questions and would be available to the legal department of our franchise if we made any progress in selling the master franchise. Over the next two days during some intense headache producing discussions, we would find out.

We went to an interesting place to eat with Marta and Maria. Marta spoke no English and Maria fairly well, and we spent the rest of the day telling them about how homecare worked in America. Maria listened but became very skeptical about our marketing ideas and strategy. Maybe if we had hired a translator I could have explained the business ideas more clearly. I was learning that it was best to have a professional translator with you to communicate exactly what you meant. Natalie and I got very frustrated when Maria kept saying the Russian word for no, pronounced NYET. "Nyet! Nyet! Nyet! Won't work in Russia! Nyet! Nyet! Nyet!" Truthfully, it would work in Russia, a potential gold mine, and she reluctantly agreed to some of the basic principles and began to see how it might possibly succeed.

If they bought the franchise, Anna and I would be paid a commission by our franchisor and consulting fee and Anna would come over and spend a month training them and then be available by Skype. We would also receive a small ongoing percentage of the royalties that they paid. When we talked about price, which was very fair, they said they would see if they could come up with the funds, which they had told us before that they already had (more about this later).

The next morning, we went with them to visit a Russian Orthodox cathedral that Marta had finished with the gold leaf process, which fascinated Natalie and me. I had never been to Orthodox or Catholic churches except for funerals and weddings and never one this elaborate. We had many Catholics clients in the homecare business who prayed with and for us, and in this cathedral, there were many people going to various stations and praying for different needs and lighting candles. Even though it was very unfamiliar, I truly sensed the presence of God, and it was so inspiring to see worship back in a country where it had been forbidden for so many years.

We decided we would begin to have Skype meetings with them with Arman translating when we went back to Memphis. That night they took us to The Hard Rock Café for dinner, which had recently opened in Moscow, and I spent time talking to the manager who was from London. I told him about what we were doing in Moscow and asked him if he would be interested in some form of music exchange with the popular Russian bands and possibly some of the Memphis Blues groups. He liked the idea. Having visited Memphis and being very familiar with the blues scene on Beale Street, he promised to stay in touch.

The next morning, a friend of Arman's, Albert, whom he attended Moscow State University with years ago, picked us up for the next phase of our trip. We went to brunch with him, his wife and sister-in-law and spent time getting acquainted, and they took us on a private tour of the Kremlin. His sister-in-law was the Kazakh ambassador to France at the time and had relationships with Russian government officials. We learned a lot about Soviet history and viewed vaults storing past rulers crowns, jewels, and even chunks of gold.

They took us on the subway which was massive with long escalators that led to the trains deep underground. The ceilings and walls were covered with beautiful tiles, and impressive chandeliers with multicolored glass hung from the ceilings. There were hundreds of people everywhere moving at a brisk pace. Before arriving, I had imagined Russians in drab clothes standing around in bread lines, but they looked like Americans in New York City! Albert's two daughters joined us, and thankfully they locked arms with Natalie and me so we wouldn't get separated and lost in the crowd.

Next, they treated us to one of Russia's first chain restaurants which had all types of good food (wasn't forced to eat horse meat). After dinner, they took us to an old prominent theatre and seated us on the front row where we saw a famous Russian dance troupe. The next morning they picked us up and took us to a satellite branch of Moscow University where there was a gathering of about seventy-five professors and students waiting for our business training presentation. We stressed that we would teach ESL based on business and that we would let them have hands-on experience with an American business in their particular field. They seemed impressed with the PowerPoint presentation, which Armon had translated into Russian and also with pictures of the nice downtown Memphis apartments, which we had made arrangements for their stay. Three of them committed to come and promised to spread the word. We set up a commission deal for each person they recruited and were thrilled with the outcome of the meeting.

Albert was a physician and had developed a device that enables patients to breath high altitude mountain air which he was marketing in Russia, Europe, China, and Canada. This product is supposed to treat a number of illnesses, and we talked about a way to market it in the states and added it to our list of projects.

During our time with this family, they hosted us at their city home for a couple of days, and then we traveled to their summer place about an hour and a half outside Moscow, located in a hilly area covered with old pine. Many of the affluent live in the city and go to this forest on weekends and holidays. It was a very old two-story log cabin with fancy hand-carved woodwork and a gigantic fireplace. It was late January and there was about a foot of snow on the ground in Moscow, and we enjoyed some fairly mild temperatures for Russia, so they said. But when we got to the forest the daytime highs were around ten degrees with a strong breeze, and we learned the true meaning of the word COLD.

On our last day, they treated us with what they called a Russian Orthodox feast, which began with a vodka toast. About forty-five minutes later, we had another and forty-five minutes later, another. Albert said that the three toasts represented The Father, The Son and the Holy Ghost (hmmm). Vodka was very important to that culture and they believed it was the perfect cure for almost anything that ails you. Albert's wife clipped off a root of a special plant that was soaking in vodka on the window seal and put it into a plastic baggy. She told me to plant it and when it grew, to clip off some of the roots and soak them in vodka for six months. She sheepishly smiled and winked at me and said, "If you take a sip of the finished product daily it will make you superman and Anna would be thrilled forever!"(no comment). They were a wonderful family and we couldn't have asked for more gracious hosts.

Next, it was off to the airport, and when we arrived, Albert's daughter, who drove us, said she might be able to get us on an earlier flight. She went to the check-in counter and remarkably, got us on a flight that was taking off shortly. I struggled going through security as usual with taking off my shoes, my belt, taking out my laptop and cell phone, and Natalie was more than eager to get back home, to say the least. It was the last call to get on the plane, and Natalie was getting frustrated watching me and blurted out, "Dad, I'm getting on the plane!" She took off jogging toward our gate, and I made it right before they closed the door (whew).

CHAPTER 5

※※※

Get off the Porch and Run with the Big Dogs

$\mathcal{W}$e arrived back in Memphis, with our luggage coming two weeks later, excited about the possibilities and much work to do. We needed a physical office instead of meeting at Starbucks or at our homecare office. Arman had moved into a nice apartment provided by a Mississippi cotton farmer he had translated for in Uzbekistan, and the complex was owned by the farmer's son. They also wanted to help him get back on his feet. We decided to work from his apartment and make it our office.

Arman had been living with his sister whose husband was in prison in Uzbekistan for speaking out against government atrocities. Our first project was to prepare for the business training program, since we already had the first students committed from Russia. We decided to lease another apartment in Arman's complex to accommodate future students, which we fully furnished. We found a great business ESL teacher, a Memphis tour guide, a marketing firm and an attorney to work with us. Two of the students had acquired marketing degrees and the other was a lawyer, and our plan was to let the marketing students spend time with the marketing firm and the lawyer spent time with one of my attorney friends.

Anna was returning from her last trip from India and spent time with Arman working out the logistics of the trip. Natalie was going to supervise the girls and keep them entertained and was creating a fun schedule for them. I was spending time in our home-care business and having meetings with Arman who was staying up late talking to our partners in Kazakhstan on Skype. Their time was exactly the opposite, twelve hours different, and we weren't able to communicate with them until about 10 pm our time. Most of them didn't start their business day until 10:00 or 11:00 a.m. On my trips to Kazakhstan, I would usually touch base with Anna about 9:00 a.m. Kazak time and to the kids when they were available. At 9:00 p.m. their time I would talk to my office manager with the homecare business and find out how the previous day went and help put out fires if need be. Then I would talk to Arman and work out the details for my next day in Kazakhstan and he was also on-call round the clock if I needed him. Thank God for Skype because it was free and we could actually look at each other in real-time. It was so good to see Anna's face almost every day and be encouraged and assured that we were doing the right thing having to spend so much time apart.

I was leaving in a few weeks to go back to Nicaragua to do another baseball camp with the coach. This was my first love, but I truly was starting to believe that God was also calling me to do mission work through business to make a lot of money for the Kingdom. Anna and I had decided that we were going to live as modest a lifestyle as possible and give the rest away. I thought we had enough money to live on forever, especially if our new venture took off. We were getting the homecare business ready to sell because I was burned out and didn't have the zeal to take it to the next level. I didn't think much about the $10,000 a month flying out the window with Natalie and Reid in college, paying for all of our cars, cell phones, insurance, and nice home in Lakeland. We also had an old 4,500 square feet house we had bought and remodeled for our growing homecare office which had to have more space. We added a few bathrooms and were housing students from a school of worship arts that our church had started. I had begun to pay Arman a salary and bought him a late model Ford Expedition which had enough space to carry our visitors and made a good first impression when we picked them up at the airport.

We were receiving more offers for commodity deals in Russia, as word got out, and there was an opportunity to make millions. The training class was scheduled for late summer, and we had all of our ducks in a row. Reid was out of school for the summer, and along with Natalie, was beginning to take Russian language lessons from Arman who had convinced them that learning that language would open many doors in the future.

Reid was writing bios of our business team and was able to make us look impressive. He was also designing marketing materials and stories for Natalie to place on our website, which was up and running. After watching all the stress Anna and I experienced, neither of them wanted any part of our family homecare business. Natalie had worked in the office running QuickBooks and making daily bank deposits after high school classes and saw the operations up close. She also did marketing distributing brochures to our referral sources, and she saw firsthand what running it entailed.

When I returned from the baseball camp (very rewarding and fun), we met with Jimmy, the elderly fellow from church who had given me the mazut proposal. We had received feedback from Erkin and Alamut, and the prices weren't in line with what China was looking for, so we began negotiations and got closer.

Jimmy got Arman and me on the phone with his connection, James, in the oil business who had given him the proposal. James turned out to be a wonderful person, and we are still friends to this day. He was a wealthy retired gentleman in his early seventies and had the time and money to look for these deals. He was from southeast Texas and made his fortune in the timber industry and had a lot of experience in international business. He had sold timber products to several European countries and at one time had shipped more telephone poles to Mexico than anyone. He was a fun-loving, upbeat, former college quarterback and someone I looked up to and trusted, who was also a Baptist minister. I learned a lot about negotiating from him by watching him on a couple of later visits to Kazakhstan. He had buyers for different commodities in the States and in China and was delighted to have opportunities in the former Soviet Union. China didn't buy directly from Russia and went through brokers who took temporary ownership and then sold the products. We planned a visit for him to come to Memphis and brainstorm how to make headway.

Now it was late spring of 2010 and time for our first business class to arrive from Moscow, and one of the girls suddenly backed out. We had charged a reasonable fee and the other two arrived with cash, but with one of the girls not coming, we barely made enough to cover expenses because we hadn't thought to get a deposit. We got them settled in, and they were eager to see the sights and sounds of Memphis. Natalie took them to dinner and out and about, and this was to eventually wear Natalie out. Neither of them wanted to go back to the apartment at a reasonable hour, and Natalie became their designated driver, and boy those girls could party! We determined we had to set limits for the next class on the entertainment part because it almost got out of hand.

The first morning began with Arman talking about business practices in Russia, and I followed up with how it worked here. Next, I talked to them about starting and owning a business and how it was our plan for them to go back and set up an office in Moscow to be our agents while working on their own projects. Next, the lady we hired for the ESL class came in, although both of these girls spoke good English. We found that many of the upper class in Russia and Central Asia spoke English with a British accent because their parents would send them to London in their mid-teens to master the language. Our class was teaching them to know the business lingo, so they could understand exactly what we were communicating in order to work deals. Each day the marketing student would spend time at a prominent Memphis marketing and advertising firm, mostly learning how we did things on the internet. She would also spend time with one of my salespeople in homecare. He took her on calls with him and was a master at networking. She was amazed at how all the folks he called on he had made friends with and actually enjoyed him stopping by. This was a fairly new concept in Russia. We introduced the law student to an attorney that I had known from high school and had handled legal matters for me for years. He allowed her to sit in on depositions and introduced her to a civil court judge who let her visit her chamber and sit in on several trials. We definitely needed an attorney in Russia, and she seemed excited to fill that role.

The next part of our class was to have a pastor friend of mine come in and teach about relating to and working with different cultures and religions. This was also a way to share what we believed in a nonthreatening and constructive way. He ended up not being able to make it for the session, so Anna and I addressed the subject.

Natalie and Reid introduced the students to some of their friends and tried their best to model to them how young people socialize here. Natalie and Reid have good people skills and thank God both of them behaved better than I did at their age. I am so grateful that they have chosen responsible friends (for the most part). The girls seemed like they learned something and enjoyed our culture and committed to go back home and start working with us. They were also going to recruit other students for the training class for a nice fee.

When they left, we had another promising meeting with Jimmy. I mentioned the artifacts and asked if his China connection, who he and James had worked with for a few years, might be interested. He introduced me to David who owned two popular Chinese restaurants in Memphis. He was a savvy businessman who I remain good friends with. I showed him the CD Erkin had given me with pictures and descriptions of all the artifacts. He mentioned he had a good friend that had a museum filled with ancient Hebrew and Chinese relics. David took a copy of the CD and stopped by and showed it to him. He was interested in one of the artifacts, but we couldn't come to an agreement with our Kazakh dealer on the price.

I had been searching for someone with ties to the professional boxing community to explore opportunities that I had promised to the promoter in Almaty. I remembered, Paul, who I had played baseball against in college and also had a little extracurricular fun with years ago. He was selling commercial real estate and had been a sports agent and boxing promoter. I met him with his boss, who also turned out to be a friend of one of my close business contacts. He had heard about some of our business activities and came along because he had been dabbling in overseas natural gas ventures. I asked Paul, "Can you arrange some fights in Memphis with boxers in Central Asia and Russia?"

He grinned and said, "For sure, that's a no-brainer." Then he looked at me with a smirk on his face and asked, "Aren't you the guy that missed the five-yard field goal against us in high school?"

I said, "You're still a smartass aren't you?" I had forgotten that I also played football against him, and he was on that opposing team that I will never forget.

Paul scheduled a meeting with a very colorful character that occasionally hosts pro fights at his theatre on Beale Street. He said that he thought it would be a wonderful idea and was interested. Paul and this fellow put some numbers together and Paul came back and said that with everything that was involved it would be impossible for us to make any money on the fights, so we decided to pursue it from another angle. Paul said he left the promoting business because of the corruption and the cutthroat business practices. Arman called his friend in Almaty and told him that we were still working on it, and had to come up with a different plan. We actually found a different solution the next time I went back to Almaty with several other interesting characters.

James, from Texas, came to Memphis and we spent time with him, David and Jimmy, getting to know each other. David had received several more offers for mazut and crude oil from China and he had been working with James for several years on different ventures there. Arman had received news from Amina, the hotel manager's mother, that she had another source for the mazut with much better pricing. Even though she was good friends with Erkin, we found them competing with each other, and we made plans to meet with her. Also, Paul had a source for very high-end Italian ladies shoes that he helped design. I found it hard to believe that an old north Memphis ballplayer had that type of artistic talent, but he showed me pictures of him and his partner receiving an award in Vegas. He also had top of the line apparel sources in Italy from where his parents had immigrated to the states in the thirties. Paul played professional baseball there for ten years and still had many contacts in that part of the world. He actually played baseball for the Italian baseball team in the LA Olympics. He said that players on the USA team were surprised when he answered them with a very American southern drawl. Amina, in Almaty, had a connection who we later rented an apartment and office from, who was a government official who oversaw apparel imports. She was looking for authentic ladies' goods that weren't knockoffs from China. Almaty, being two hundred miles from the border of China, was flooded with all sorts of counterfeit products. Paul's boss was also looking for a perfect place to put a hotel.

I had a fairly large list of projects to work on and took off on my second trip to Kazakhstan. It was the end of the summer in 2010, and I would spend ten days. Amina picked me up at the airport and took me to the Holiday Inn where her daughter was the manager. It was very expensive, and the next day we spent time looking for a more practical place to stay. Her apparel friend had a three-bedroom place for lease in a gated secure building decorated with gold leaf like Marta produced in Moscow, which was prominent in some of the nicer homes. It seemed to be a status symbol for the wealthy, and it covered all the trim and crown mold. Paul was planning to join me on the next trip if I thought the opportunities and deals were real. His company would eventually share the cost, and we rented it together for the next two years. We learned that a lot of international commodity deals are fake, and one of my purposes was to find out if these people had the connections that they claimed they had.

That afternoon, I met with Oraz who would be the seller side broker on the mazut and other oil products. He was a nice-looking, small, slender Kazakh man with long coal-black hair in his early forties. Arman had emailed him some of our offers from James, Jimmy's contact, and he assured us that he had located the products. Before we could proceed and hopefully make progress, we had to work out the commissions. Usually, there is a buyer and seller side commission based on plats, which is an international trading scale that changes based on the daily price of the commodity. It takes all the guesswork out of what the price will be. It all comes down to the commission the buyer and seller are willing to pay and is split by everyone who has a piece of the pie on each end of the deal.

Later that day, Oraz and I jumped on Skype with Arman, who seemed comfortable with Oraz, and they begin to talk late nearly every night, our time, about the prospects. The next morning Amina took me to meet with her apparel contact who had leased us the apartment. She had a very nice store with expensive brands and was also overseeing other stores in Almaty. I gave her a brochure with Paul's shoes and showed her his internet site. He had actually won an award for the best new shoe design a few years earlier and she saw this on his website and was very impressed.

I met with Alamut the next day and we discussed the Angus beef opportunity he had mentioned, and I told him I had a connection, who was also Paul, whose brother was in the business. He gave me the specs of exactly what he was looking for, and Paul and his brother went to work.

I had the next few days open and decided that I would look for business contacts on my own. The Noodles café proved to be a perfect place to meet businessmen from all over the world. I spent a few days hanging out there and anybody I overheard speaking English with any kind of accent, I would simply and quickly introduce myself and give them a business card. I would tell them to check out our website and if they thought we could help each other make money to give me a call or email me. I had bought an inexpensive phone at the Dubai airport on my connecting flight. That phone allowed me to buy a card with local minutes for a very cheap price, and ten dollars covered that trip and my next. Before I left the café, Carsten, a young man from Denmark, walked over to me and said he checked out the website and had some ideas. He proved to be the best contact that I met on any of my trips to Almaty. We worked on many different deals, and he later came to Houston to meet James and his major oil contact (more about that later).

On my walk back to the apartment which was just a couple of blocks from Noodles, I took a different route and noticed a huge complex, Kimep University. I decided I would go in and see if they might be interested in our business training program. I walked up to the information desk and asked if I could speak to someone who spoke English, and the greeter explained to me that it was a university that offered North American accredited courses and that all of the classes were taught in English! She was a pretty, college-aged girl. One of the first things that I had noticed was the very beautiful ladies everywhere that I went (more about that later). I told her my purpose for the visit, and she took me on a long stroll across campus and introduced me to the person in charge of programs like ours. I had a wonderful conversation with her, and she said she could set up a meeting with interested faculty. She said it would take a little time to schedule and would be in touch. I told her I was leaving shortly, and she called me that night and said that she would be able to schedule it the next day with some professors during an afternoon break. I went with some literature and the PowerPoint presentation that Natalie had put together. I had a frustrating, stressful moment connecting to their internet with a few of them glaring at me but finally got connected. The presentation was easy because they all spoke English, and I didn't have to speak through a translator and could use the English version. Arman had converted the slide show to Russian if need be. What I remember most was the question and answer session at the end. An instructor from France asked me, "Will you be the one teaching the ESL classes?"

I said, "No, it won't be me."

He laughed and said, "Good, we don't want them coming back sounding like country hicks."

There seemed to be some interest, and I spoke with them several times when I returned home to hopefully get something started.

CHAPTER 6

※

Don't Be a Topwater, Go down There Deep with the Sharks

I thought it had been a productive time in Almaty and headed back to Memphis to follow up with these deals. Anna was meeting with women's groups and Russian teachers in Memphis and was having a blast and would take Arman along. He was very well-spoken and handsome, and the ladies were always very impressed with him. Rhodes College had the largest Russian curriculum with several Russian professors, and Arman immediately hit it off with them. He had a doctorate in agriculture and had also been a university professor in Uzbekistan. They began planning different cultural exchange projects, mainly art and music, and Anna was in wholeheartedly.

It was September 2010 and we were making plans for my next visit to Almaty, and it was to be a longer stay, about thirty days. The first week Paul would join me and bring samples of his shoes and give Alamut a proposal for the beef. Arman had someone else he wanted me to meet, Talgat, who he said had oil contacts and a better idea about the boxing venture. I was planning on spending time with Carsten and introducing him to Paul. We also had Skype meetings scheduled with Oraz, Arman, and our future partner from Texas about oil prospects.

I took off again for Almaty through Amsterdam this time. I had connecting flights through all these cool places, but all I could do was hang out in the airports. Paul arrived in Almaty the day after me, and he had spent many hours working on his beef proposal which involved different cuts than were sold in the US. He was on the phone with our American trade rep in Almaty and customs officials and vendors for refrigerated shipping containers. Paul had arrived with a very nice presentation with catalogs of colorful pictures of each cut of beef with detailed pricing.

We met Alamut at Noodles the next day for brunch. Alamut spoke English and there was no need for a translator, and he asked if he could make a vodka toast. We accepted (11:00 a.m.) and later figured out that these toasts were more than an age-old tradition. It was also a technique they used in negotiations to hopefully get you to be more flexible or to give up the contact at your source. They would also have to feel like they were totally screwing you in the deal. They were never going to be happy with a win-win situation like in the west where everybody can make money. They had to think that they won and you lost. We found out that most Kazakhs didn't hold their liquor very well and seemed affected by just two toasts. We had a nice buffet (no horse meat). Paul asked Alamut about his family, and he told us his father was a military officer and ran a training facility about an hour away from town. He said they practiced with tanks and handheld bazookas, etc. He said that maybe he could take us out there sometime and we could blow some stuff up (I'm not kidding) and we told him that would be a lot of fun. I saw the place on my next trip with another contact and it was acres and acres of brick buildings that definitely had been shot at with something more powerful than bullets. Then we got down to business and Alamut was impressed by the catalog that Paul was going through. Then he hesitated when he saw the prices and busted out laughing and sarcastically said, "I can buy meat cheaper than that in the grocery store."

Paul was very jet-lagged and didn't get much sleep when he arrived and was visibly upset. This was a negotiating technique that Arman had warned me about. He said you had to leave your emotions out of the conversations because they would certainly try your patience. After hearing this remark, Paul excused himself for a minute. I asked Alamut, "Are you willing to pay more for the beef?"

He said, "Sure."

Paul came back after he cooled off and had made a call to his brother (1:00 a.m. US time). We were able to shave a little off the price, but Alamut said it wasn't acceptable and asked us to see what we could do to get the price down further. That was the end of the meeting and the price couldn't be lowered any more without us losing our share of the deal. Paul was very angry and discouraged, and I gave him my best pep talk and got him back to his comical self.

We spent time with Carsten later that day, and he told Paul not to give up on the beef idea because he knew some of the high-end restaurant owners. He had become acquainted with them from being on the board of the American Chamber of Commerce in Almaty. Carsten ran a branch of an international logistics company, his main customer being John Deere Tractor, and he was responsible for getting the equipment shipped to Russia and Central Asia.

Amina picked us up to meet her clothing contact, and Paul had samples of his shoes, and she was very impressed and didn't object too much with the price. She assured us that she would place an order in the near future.

That evening, we went to dinner with Carsten who mentioned that he had contacts at one of the prominent oil companies in Russia. One project in which he was involved in Almaty was earthquake-proofing buildings and some in Western China. A huge fault ran along the border, and he showed me pictures of the technology and how it worked. The major reason for this was because of an earthquake that had destroyed much of Almaty in 1911 (first I had heard about that). He said most of the city was rebuilt with cheap building materials and poor structure design from China that could never withstand an earthquake like the previous one. He knew that Memphis and areas of California were ripe for earthquakes. Carsten had a home in Almaty and another in Belarus where his wife was born and raised. They had two young children, and Carsten brought his son to Noodles to meet me on a later visit. He said he was bringing his business manager and then showed up with his handsome boy who he introduced as his boss. His wife was becoming increasingly nervous in Almaty and couldn't get over her fear of another earthquake. This technology fascinated Paul because it was practical, fairly easy to install, and wasn't terribly expensive. Paul's real estate company managed apartments in San Francisco and all over the States and, of course, in Memphis, and he spent time when he returned marketing this product in areas that were in danger of earthquakes.

The next day, Amina and her clothing associate took us sightseeing, and it was early fall and they took us up a scenic mountain drive. It was about eighty-five degrees in the city with a climate similar to Memphis with lingering hot days. You could take a twenty-minute drive and the temperature would drop to around sixty-five degrees on a road that ran adjacent to a roaring river with regional ethnic restaurants along the route. Many of the wealthier people made it their daily lunch destination. You could sit outside and eat on decks that jutted out over the river, and each seat had a blanket you could wrap around your shoulders if you got chilly. Amina mentioned to Paul that she possibly had a contact for his beef with the Russian military and took one of Paul's catalogs. He left to go back to Memphis encouraged about his shoe deal and Carsten's earthquake project and maybe a longshot with his Angus beef. The boxing promoter was out of town which was a relief for us because we didn't have any good news for him.

In my nightly call with Anna, she said that she had heard back from the ladies in Moscow, Marta and Maria, with whom we had tried to set up the master homecare franchise. They said they definitely could not come up with the funds but still wanted to get into the business. They asked Anna if we could help for a fee, and I knew we would first have to clear this idea with our franchise. I hung up the phone and called him, and he said that he was planning on reaching me and telling me that, since the ladies were having so many issues with our ways of doing things, that it wouldn't be a good idea. Their legal team had also thought it would be too hairy doing this type of business in Russia. I asked them if we could help them get something going on their own and they said that it would be okay with certain conditions and he emailed me a list of trade secrets not to be shared with them. Anna was excited about this and began planning her first trip to Moscow. She had become friends with the girls that had been here for the training program and would hopefully be able to encourage their progress working with us and help them in recruiting new students.

I had two weeks remaining in Almaty and spent the next few days exploring the city by walking in a different direction each day and keeping my eyes open for contacts in the businesses lining the streets. I discovered that there was an informal Uber-type service there. You would simply stand on a corner and stick up your thumb, and someone would pick you up. Many people that lived on the outskirts of Almaty who had cars did this for a living, and most of them didn't speak English, and I was assured by my contacts that it was safe.

I had met a young man at Noodles from China who was already running an online version of our business training program and met with him one of those afternoons. It was about an hour until my appointment with him, so I thought I would give it a try. I stuck up my thumb and within a minute or two a young fellow picked me up. He didn't speak very good English so I decided to call my Chinese friend and give him the phone. My new contact directed us straight to the address with no problem which was about a fifteen-minute drive and cost the equivalent of three American dollars. I used this mode of transportation many times on my next visits and never had a problem. On the return trip, I would just say, "Kazakhstan Hotel" and all of them understood and knew where it was, just a short walk from my apartment. I had a nice discussion with the Chinese man, and we made a commitment to finding ways to work with each other.

My next appointment was a Skype call with Oraz, Arman, and James, and we agreed to have it at 9 that night. Oraz and his crew arrived at about ten, and it reminded me of something that I noticed about their culture. If you weren't five minutes early, Kazakhs would appear to be disgusted with you. James had told us that he had secured a letter of credit to purchase the product they offered. As we were discussing the project on our Skype call, Oraz asked James with Arman translating, "Are you prepared to complete the other two offers that were on the table?"

James hesitated and told him, "We will only be able to do one at a time because of the amount of money."

Oraz was very upset and angrily replied, "You promised that you could do all the deals."

Amina had brought her banker along and evidently told him that it was going to be a huge transaction (they were counting the money they assumed was already theirs). That abruptly ended the conversation and I was very confused, to say the least, about what had just transpired. Arman told Oraz that we would work on the other letters of credit and the Skype call was finished.

Oraz then looked at me with a very agitated expression, and I walked out on the balcony for a minute to try to wrap my head around what had just transpired. Amina had brought a young family friend of hers and Oraz's to translate. They soon followed me outside and Oraz began to speak in a harsh tone. The translator said, "Oraz wants you to look at him when he speaks."

I looked up at Oraz. He told me through the translator, "You are a liar! You told me James could do all the deals."

This infuriated me and I said something in a low voice, neglecting Arman's advice about keeping emotions out of it. Oraz asked me firmly, "What did you say?"

I responded trying to keep my composure, "I don't appreciate you calling me a liar!" I tried to explain to him in detail why James couldn't do the deals simultaneously. I'm glad the translator didn't understand my first remark because I told him, "Tell that little pecker wood that if he calls me a liar again I'm going to toss him over the rail!" (Oraz, being a tiny fellow.)

Oraz then lightened up and said through the translator, "I was actually kidding." He obviously wasn't.

I smiled, shook his hand, and said, "We need to work together because we are on the same team." Arman, James, and I decided that would be the last time we worked with them on commodity deals. I didn't tell them that because Amina's shoe buyer seemed authentic, and we didn't want to burn that bridge. Wow, what a night!

Carsten had mentioned to me that he had doubts about some of the Kazakhs we were working with and said that they really didn't understand international business. He said we should work directly with legitimate brokers who had proven experience working with Russia. We eventually took his word and followed his advice after it proved true again with several deals falling apart wasting mega amounts of money and time. All of these funds were coming out of Anna and my, Paul and his boss's, and James's pockets since we were all financing our own expenses.

We were soon to be greatly encouraged over the next ten days meeting and working with Arman's contact Talgat. He picked me up the next Monday morning in a nice SUV and even offered me one of his other vehicles to drive, but I knew my insurance wouldn't cover it (he said he didn't have any). He had an office in Almaty with the Russian government and worked closely with the Israeli Embassy. He was also a former Russian professional boxer and was a big dominating dude about my age. He spoke with the British accent that I mentioned before and was also working with Olympic and amateur boxing in Kazakhstan. He showed me a few of his favorite places in the mountains driving into snow-capped areas with some of the most beautiful views I had ever seen. He showed me venues being prepared for the winter Asian Olympics and told me with a smile on his face, "Corrupt Almaty government officials have already spent most of the allotted money on personnel ventures. Much of this won't be completed." When I went back in the winter, he was proven to be right, and they had moved some events to other cities. He took me skiing on a future trip (very interesting and not safe for rookie skiers like myself).

After turning me on to some of his favorite places in the mountains, he took me to a restaurant owned by a friend of his. When we went in, he introduced me to another giant whose name was Mikel. He was a former Russian heavyweight boxing champion, and I remembered watching him fight in the 1996 Olympics in Atlanta where they had to stop the fight in the finals because of a gash over his eye. I mentioned the boxing exchange idea, and he was very interested and invited me to some matches the next morning.

It was a special event honoring Kazakh boxers who had won gold medals for Russia in former Soviet days. We walked into a gymnasium and there were boxers from different Central Asian countries warming up with all the different Stans present and even North Korea. I stopped by and watched the North Korean group for a minute wondering if they would be a somber bunch (kept on leashes or something) but they seemed happy and were joking around with their coach. Talgat and Mikel took me to the scorer's table and introduced me to a famous referee who had officiated Olympic and professional boxing for thirty years, and they invited me to sit with them. I watched a couple of fights and then a heavyweight match between North Korea and Kyrgyzstan which was evidently a big rivalry. At the end of the fights, they honored the former Kazakh gold medal winners, and then they surprised me by allowing me to assist in placing medals on the winners of the day's fights.

Mikel asked me on the way back to the restaurant if I was interested in arranging a match with the Kazakh Olympic team and the American team. I told him that I would get in touch with my partner Paul and see if we could make it happen. I talked with Paul on Skype that night, and he said it was possible, especially because he was a former Olympian and had the connections. I was fired up, to say the least, and couldn't wait to tell Anna.

The next day Talgat wanted me to meet his ex-wife Sofia who still worked with him and appeared to be his best friend. She was former KGB and currently worked on Pakistani and Afghan affairs. She claimed that she advised the Kremlin and our defense department on the war effort in Afghanistan. At the time, Russia and our government were cooperating (still are) on keeping radical Islam out of the former Soviet Union. She was also involved in rebuilding trade on the former Silk Road and was deeply connected in their transportation system.

They turned me on to their favorite shish kabob place which offered beef, pork, chicken, and lamb. There were stands all over Almaty, and it was some of the best meat that I had ever tasted, which they cooked over a wood fireplace. Later we enjoyed restaurants in various parts of town, each with its own former Soviet regional cuisine. We talked about our backgrounds and hobbies and enjoyed each other's company for several days. She said that Talgat felt very comfortable with me, and she wanted to discuss a very confidential project that she was working on. She said that she understood that James had contacts in the oil business and that she had done background research on both of us. Sofia didn't speak very good English, so Talgat interpreted to make sure we understood each other. This venture involved the sale of jet fuel from Russian refineries to our air force base in Bagram, Afghanistan. It would be a contract with our Department of Defense and on a much larger scale than I could have imagined. She said that another company had acquired the uncontested contract for ten years and there was ongoing corruption on both sides, and the Russians wanted to open it up to other bidders. She mentioned that the Russian government wanted to start making changes and the bid date was the next spring. I told her I would find out if James had the government connections and financing to proceed with a deal of that scope. She also wanted to know if I had ties with FedEx who was making weekly deliveries to Almaty and how to increase those deliveries or to bring a FedEx hub to Kazakhstan. I told them that I would do some research and would be in touch on Skype and return to Almaty in a couple of months.

I went back home to Memphis with more opportunities than I could comprehend. I had never been so happy to see Anna and the kids and was so glad to be on American soil. Anna was getting ready to go to Moscow to help the ladies with their homecare business. Arman had translated business forms into Russian that would be useful to them such as employment applications, service contracts, samples of marketing material, etc. and a small employee handbook, and Anna was as excited as I had ever seen her.

CHAPTER 7

><><

The Hangover

$\mathcal{W}$e were both concerned about our time away from each other and the kids, but Natalie and Reid seemed to be thriving. The church where we were in ministry had moved to another part of town, and we decided to keep a branch of the church in Lakeland with members who didn't want to make the move and began meeting at our home. I was paying Reid to lead worship and Natalie to work with the kids. It fizzled out quickly because I was the only one really thrilled about it, and we were traveling too much to be available to meet the needs of the group.

Anna and I agreed that we were being led to pursue missions through business and continued to pursue the calling. Our homecare business was doing well but not growing as fast as it had the previous year. We had qualified staff running it and attributed the slow down to the economy.

Arman had been in touch with James about the Russian jet fuel deal, and his partner said we would have to bring in someone else that could handle the financial end. He had been the vice president of a major oil company and was part of the first drilling operations of an American firm in Russia. He agreed to work with us, and James flew to Memphis to begin the planning. James's partner, Jimmy, said that he had a relative who was a retired senator, JB, from Tennessee who had contacts with the DOD. He could support us with the legal work and place us in line for the bidding process in the spring and also be a well-known reference for us.

We formed a joint venture, and Reid created a portfolio with pictures and bios. Arman translated it into Russian, so we would have English and Russian versions, which Natalie posted on our website. We printed copies to take to Sofia and Talgat when we returned to Almaty in the fall, where Sofia would explain in great detail how we could work together and discuss the complicated logistics and pricing.

Paul had been in touch with the US Olympic Committee, and there happened to be a representative nearby in Jackson, TN who agreed to meet with us for lunch at a popular Memphis restaurant. Paul invited his colorful promoter friend from Beale Street to join us to find about using his venue for the matches. Paul told the committee rep that they would need to write a letter of invitation to the Kazakh team, which we would hand deliver. This was standard procedure and would also prove whether the Kazakhs were serious. There were many details to work out as far as transportation and lodging, how much we would charge, and how the gate money would be divided. Paul's friend said we could use his facility for free and that all he wanted was the concessions, which included alcohol. The committee lady from Jackson said no alcohol was allowed at any of their matches, so Paul's friend backed out, and we would have to find another facility. We agreed to try to make it happen no later than February of the next year because any time later would be too close to the upcoming Olympics. It was late October 2010, so we had to get busy. Paul had a friend with the casino operations in Tunica who mentioned a separate venue for indoor sporting events, and they could prohibit the sale of alcohol. He agreed to let us use the building for a small fee for security with an EMT and ambulance on site.

The boxing and jet fuel deals seemed very hopeful, and we were certain that they would come to fruition, and the plan was to go back to Almaty in mid-November. James would stay with me for a week and meet with Talgat and Sofia, and Paul would come the next week and bring the letter of invitation to the boxers. Also, Paul had been in touch with Amina's contact with the apparel business, our new landlord, and she asked Paul for some more samples of shoes that she believed would sell.

My mother was eighty-one and recovering from a seriously broken hip and was having complications. Anna was still in Moscow, and Natalie and I were checking on her every day. She had one of our caregivers with her round the clock for a couple of months, and I was debating whether I should go back to Almaty, but my mother insisted I go. When Anna came back from Moscow, she would be there with Natalie to make sure that her needs were met.

Anna's trip turned out to be unsuccessful in getting the Russian homecare business started. She said Maria kept objecting to all the ideas about how to run the business and again kept saying that it wouldn't work in Russia. Since they said it wouldn't succeed, they didn't believe they owed us any money except for Anna's room and board, but Anna stayed positive and didn't burn any bridges. She spent the last week with Albert and his family and had fun sightseeing in Moscow but didn't make progress with the training class project.

Natalie kept busy maintaining our website and struggling with statistics in college. She persevered and eventually got through it. Reid was in his second year of college at another Memphis school and was in the process of transferring to Knoxville to the university there. Everything seemed to be going well with our family.

Here we go again to Almaty, and things got a little crazy this time (more than a little). James arrived shortly after I did and after a little sleep, I took him to Noodles. One of the staff saw us walking around the side of the Kazakhstan hotel, and several of them ran up to greet us. I had spent a lot of time there and enjoyed hanging out with them, who were mostly young girls around Natalie's age who she had met on the first trip. They would always have American coffee waiting and a table saved, if they knew I was coming. I had told Carsten that James was coming, and they enjoyed visiting at Noodles. Carsten was to meet us in Houston the next year to do a deal with wood chips from a Texas mill with a large Russian company. They used this type of wood for heating in much of the former Soviet Union.

Later that afternoon, we met Talgat and Sofia, and they spent some time chatting with James. He had brought Talgat a Stetson cowboy hat and a nice cowgirl belt for Sofia. James was my favorite guest because he would never let me pay for anything. On any of our future trips, if I would pay for any of our meals or group meals, he would slip a hundred dollar bill in my back pocket. They were eager to show James around, and the next day they took us to some places that I hadn't seen before.

Afterward, they took us to a Turkish restaurant, and we went to a private room and began to discuss the jet fuel deal. Sofia had a friend that worked with the current supplier, the Russian refineries that were supplying the fuel to our air force bases in Kyrgyzstan and Afghanistan. They had a ten-year ongoing contract with a company run by an American in California. He was supposedly skimming money and fuel off the deal for private use. The suspected corruption was between this man and the president of Kyrgyzstan and several US Congressmen, and Congress was investigating the matter. Sofia said the new plan would involve shipping the fuel by train to the Kazakhstan border and then trucking the fuel to Begran instead of from our base in Kyrgyzstan. They were having bottleneck problems in that area and were sometimes having to transfer fuel from Russian planes to our planes in the air. I seemed a little skeptical about this, and she showed me pictures of it taking place. After a couple of days of discussions, we determined how to split the commissions if the deal took place.

When James returned home, we began to create some draft contracts to finalize our method of working together, and Sofia emailed us a copy of the DOD contract that had been used for the past ten years. We would serve as the broker and purchase the product from her refineries and then sell to the DOD, which was standard procedure. The past ten-year renewing contracts had amounted to about one billion dollars (gulp).

James returned to Texas and Paul arrived a few days later and the plan was for Amina to pick up Paul and me for lunch the next day. Paul arrived late in the afternoon and suggested we go to one of the other restaurants at the Kazakhstan Hotel. We walked the two blocks there and went in to get a table and the place was packed. We noticed other foreigners and a band from London was setting up to play. We were seated at the bar while waiting on a table. The very friendly bartender perceived we were new and offered us a free vodka toast, which we accepted. A few minutes later they seated us at a table, and the next thing I noticed was Paul moonwalking on the dance floor. Two young women were standing beside our table, and Paul walked over with a confused look on his face and reached out with his wallet and told me to take it. He almost lost his balance and the women began to make conversation with us.

The next thing that I remember was sitting on the sofa in our apartment with Paul's shoe samples scattered on the floor and the two girls trying them on. One of them was pulling on my arm and trying to get me to stand up. After that, all I recall was waking up about eleven the next morning looking in the mirror, extremely groggy, and having a beautiful, perfectly swollen black eye. I woke Paul up immediately and asked him what the heck had happened, and he was also clueless and looked at my eye with a look of shock. Shortly afterward there was a loud banging on the door and Paul opened it and there was Amina. She screamed at us angrily and said that her friend, who was our next-door neighbor, told her that there were two whores fighting in the hallway outside our door in the middle of the night. Then she looked at my eye and told me that she thought I was a Christian man and wondered what Anna would think. I was speechless and immediately called Anna and Arman and got them on the phone and did my best to explain our predicament. I told Anna my story, and she kind of chuckled and encouraged me not to worry because we trusted each other totally, and she knew there had to be a good explanation (whew).

We found out later that one of the bartenders was working with prostitutes, and this was common practice. The vodka toast was spiked! I mentioned that many of the Kazakh young girls were very pretty and fit and many of them would come in from outside the city like the drivers and hit on the foreign men, especially Americans. They would sit down very close to you in a lot of places around Almaty and put their hands under the table (yep, sure would). I had that happen several times and would just tell them firmly that I wasn't interested, and they would promptly get up and go. Some places recognized them, like Noodles, and barred them, but many didn't and engaged with them in this scheme. I told the girls at Noodles what happened and one of them looked at me and said, "Noodles, good girls. Other hotel restaurants, bad girls."

I kept ice on my eye for the rest of the day, and the next afternoon we were to meet Amina, her shoe contact, and some of her apparel associates from other stores. I remembered walking by a ladies' hair salon and stopped in first thing the next morning. I walked in and looked at the stylist and patted my eye, put up my hands, and kind of made my best "please help me" motion. They laughed and a lady stepped out from behind the counter. She spoke perfect English and sat me down and applied a lot of makeup to my face. I ended up looking like a figure in a wax museum, but it worked, and she sold me an extra bottle, and I used it for a week.

She also owned an expensive restaurant similar to Texas de Brazil and invited us to check it out and see if we had similar business interests. Paul and I went that night, and when he mentioned his Angus beef idea, she told him that the meat market was nearly impossible to break into in Almaty. It was tightly controlled by the government and the mafia, and we would lose any profit in kickbacks (great).

Before dinner that night, we met with Amina and her shoe connections. She looked at my makeup job and struggled to hold back a smile. Arman had smoothed out the ordeal, and I think she believed it wasn't our purpose to seek women like that. No one at the meeting commented on my appearance, and they tried on Paul's new shoe samples and told him they really liked them and would pursue the right market in Almaty.

The next day Talgat picked us up at 10:00 a.m., and we delivered Paul's invitation letter to the boxers. We went to their office and, Mikel, the heavyweight champion, took Paul into a side room and interviewed him. They hadn't met him or checked out his website which had photos of him playing baseball in the Olympics, pro ball in Italy, and also his Italian shoes and link to his real estate site. Talgat had informed them about Paul's real estate company's desire to build a hotel in Almaty. Mikel and Paul came out laughing and were comfortable with each other and decided to proceed.

We sat at a conference table with a huge plate of horse meat and a bottle of vodka (10:00 a.m.). Seated at the table with us were several other former boxers, and they wanted to have two toasts, one from them and one from us. You were supposed to chase the vodka with horse meat, which I forced down. Paul actually liked it having eaten it occasionally in Italy. They were really impressed with the letter of invitation and could tell it was authentic, and Mikel was looking forward to personally delivering it to the Kazakh Olympic committee in Astana, their capital city, the following week. The Kazakhs at the table poured themselves some more vodka, and Paul and I gave each other a look and were relieved we didn't have to do another toast.

They told us they wanted to take us to Big Almaty Lake, which was about an hour south of Almaty at an elevation of about eight thousand feet, glacier-fed, and surrounded by mountain peaks. There was a resort there and they wanted to expand it. Part of the plan was to build an airstrip available for private planes. They were hoping to create a Chinese tourist attraction being two hundred miles from the Chinese border and mentioned they were also looking for a hotel and a casino.

We left the office with drivers because very few of the Kazakhs drank and drove because of very severe penalties (thank God). One of the boxers riding with us passed out and was snoring loudly, and when we arrived at an amazing spot to view the lake, he stepped out of the car and stumbled and said, "Look how beautiful it is. Want to buy it?" (I promise). Next, they took us on a tour through a very small town on the lake, and we noticed several boarded-up buildings.

We stopped at a building that had a few cars parked outside to get a bite to eat and to observe. It was supposed to be a casino and had several card tables and three or four other gambling stations. In our discussion over lunch, they said that you had to spend $400 minimum. Paul asked if they had any statistics showing how much money they made daily, weekly, etc., and they said they didn't. He asked if they knew how many people came from Almaty daily, weekly, etc., and they didn't. He told them that the big draws and money makers in the US were the slot machines, but there were none here or in any of their other casinos, which all appeared to be going out of business. Their idea to solve the absence of any statistics was for us to come down one day and count the cars coming from Almaty and another day try to watch and see how much people spent in the casinos, and this astonished Paul, and he told them he would get back to them. When we were waiting for them at the car, Paul looked at me and busted out laughing and asked, "Can you believe all of this?" We realized that this country had only experienced capitalism for a very short period and had little idea of how business deals like this worked. They honestly assumed we would invest a fortune in this project and everybody would make money. Paul headed back to Memphis at least confident that the boxing was a go.

That Saturday night Talgat told me they wanted to have a special Kazakh ceremony honoring me as their new partner, and we drove out the same highway that we took to the lake. This road, I forgot to mention, was covered with large potholes like an obstacle course. On the way, he mentioned that the government was supposed to repave it in the very near future (sure they were). The ceremony was to begin with a short fishing excursion on a large river surrounded by huge cliffs. A cold wind was blowing, so we didn't take the boat but fished off the bank, and they weren't biting.

My hosts were cooking a large goat with all the trimmings, and I watched one of the boxers clean and then roast it over a fire. They made a campfire and I took a seat with several vodka toasts expressing how thrilled we were to be business partners. I had learned a trick from a friend who had done a lot of business in Russia and wasn't a drinker. He said if you are outside after two or three toasts you can start tossing them over your shoulder because they will be too drunk to know the difference (did this inside a few times). The sun was setting and I took advantage of the technique which they didn't notice or my makeup covered black eye. After the toast, they brought the head of the goat off the fire and put it onto a large platter and said that the ancient custom was for the honored guest to eat the eyeballs first (that's what they said). While I was pondering this wild idea, one of the old boxers sitting next to me plucked out an eyeball and put it promptly in my mouth. It wasn't that bad, and I plucked out the other eye and chewed it a little and swallowed it. They were all so happy and praised me and said what a good guy I was, and then they said that the ears were next and sliced one-off, which tasted okay, and then off with the other one. We shared stories, chowed down on the rest of the goat, and they drove me back to my apartment.

Tuesday morning, I received a call from Talgat and he informed me that Mikel was extremely upset and wanted to meet. I was very nervous and told Talgat that I didn't want to meet him, and I was going to get the heck out of Almaty. He talked me into reluctantly going with him to Mikel's restaurant and the minute we arrived, Mikel pointed his finger in my face and forcefully told me, "You owe me $5,000 American cash!" Then he busted out laughing. He was upset because the US committee had emailed their committee in Astana the invitation. He wanted total credit for the arrangement and I started thinking very quickly (I do that when I'm in deep dodo) I immediately had the idea for our committee to send them another letter stating that this all came about through his efforts and he was pleased. I learned soon that Olympic committees make final decisions with countries, not individuals, so I wasn't to blame.

CHAPTER 8

><|><

Nothing Like Reality

*M*y trip was cut short by some terrible news. My mother had taken a turn for the worse and I got the next flight out which ended up being my original return flight on Thursday night. I was able to spend the next ten days with her and she passed away peacefully with Anna, Natalie, and me by her side, and we are more than certain that she is in heaven. Reid was in Knoxville and came back ASAP for the service. My mom had about the greatest faith of anybody I have ever met, and if it weren't for her prayers, I would be dead or in jail (ask those that know me best).

Earlier that week, Anna told me she had something that she needed to tell me. She said she had found out a couple weeks before and knew I would rush home, so she waited and then calmly let me know that she had breast cancer! Wow! She said that they had caught it early, a very small lump, and were confident she would respond to treatment and over the next several months went through chemo, surgery and then radiation. She had a very large circle of support with many prayer warriors and friends coming alongside her. When she started chemo, we were making plans to visit James's friend in the oil business in Houston. Anna tolerated the chemo fairly well, her main side effects being exhaustion and hair loss. She also experienced tingling and burning sensations in the palms of her hands and on the soles of her feet, which lasted for at least six months.

She wasn't going to let it hold her back and remained her very spirited self. We always joked that we had never seen her sit down and how she was annoyed when the kids and myself laid around and watched TV. After each chemo treatment she would come by Arman's and help him organize the business at hand, but late every afternoon she would need to take an hour nap before she could drive back to Lakeland. We can't remember her ever napping before, and the chemo also made her very impatient because she couldn't be as active as normal. One day driving home she was in a hurry and rammed her jeep into a car on the interstate that had halted suddenly in front of her (no injuries). She was stopped three times for speeding the next few months and had her license revoked, a hefty fine, loss of her insurance, and a required driving course before getting her license reinstated. Anna is the most amazing lady that I have ever met and she wasn't going to let something like cancer thwart her activities (no way) never missing a beat.

Between the chemo and surgery, we scheduled our trip to Texas. James's friend, Jimmy, had been in touch with his former prominent Tennessee senator cousin who thought our deal would work. Over the next several months, he emailed Jimmy tips about how to proceed. He would forward these tips to us by copy and pasting the info and would sign them, Armando, for the sake of confidentiality.

James, Arman, and I met with our future financial partner, Frank, in Houston who had a very cool, ritzy setup with several nice offices and a conference room. He was retired and James's age, in his early seventies, and his passion was buying and selling oil and other commodities all over the world. He had his own attorney on staff who was also retired from the same oil company, and they would work a few days a week usually from the wee hours of the morning until around 10:00 a.m. This way they could communicate with contacts in other parts of the world in real-time. He said he enjoyed the business and was going to do it until he couldn't think straight. We met with him about 11:00 a.m., and he seemed very sleepy, but was excited about the deal and asked who our contact was with the DOD. He said that he knew a retired general who he had worked with on DOD projects but seemed comfortable with Jimmy doing the job, after learning more about him. We spent the next several hours with his secretary and attorney and added him formally to our joint venture along with Arman, James, Jimmy, and myself.

Arman and I made another same day trip back to Memphis, and I was more anxious than ever to get back home to Anna. After the chemo sessions, the tumor in her breast had shrunk considerably, but by Christmas she had lost most of her hair. On Christmas Eve I shaved her head, and she went straight to the living room with my in-laws and kids and began to show off her new style with a big broad grin (what an attitude?). The first week of January, she had a lumpectomy and removal of her lymph nodes on the right side, and the surgery went well with all signs of cancer gone. We had a glorious celebration later that week with family and friends and thanked God for the victory over the disease. We were so grateful that it was gone, and Anna started radiation ASAP, which also was successful without much pain or serious side effects.

It was early 2011, and the next step in our international business activity was to bring Sofia to Memphis to meet Anna and Arman, meet with our FedEx contact, and then head back to Houston to introduce Sofia to Frank and finalize the plan. We were still leasing the apartment for the business training program, which wasn't happening, but it would provide a comfortable place for Sofia to stay. Anna had fun showing her the sights and sounds of Memphis, and she had never experienced anything quite like Beale Street. It was her first time in America, and she was amazed at the infrastructure and how nice the native Memphians were but was shocked and surprised at the obesity she witnessed. It's not prevalent in her country because of their diet and exercise from walking instead of driving the shortest of distances like we are accustomed to. She was an attractive lady in her fifties but appeared much younger. She told us about Kazakh history and how they were nomads for centuries before Stalin rounded them up and created cities with them. Many Kazakhs hated him for persecuting their grandparents and had heard personal testimonies about his monstrosities. She said that her family was a part of the migration, along with Mongolians and other tribes of Central Asia, who came across the Bering Strait into America and became the first American Indians. The similarities are remarkable, such as their appearance and the yurts which they packed up and moved seasonally and in their languages, and it was such a fascinating history lesson.

We next had a meeting with my FedEx contact, Josh. I had met him through Kiwanis. He was retired and worked as a consultant in logistics and was instrumental in creating FedEx's ground trucking operation in the seventies, while being an original employee. He had assured me that FedEx wasn't interested in a hub in Almaty, but he could consult her on required new infrastructure needs to set up their own air freight system. Sofia said she was acquiring a grant to research improving airport and trucking systems as part of their attempt to restore the old Silk Road. She was very intrigued with Josh and his knowledge of logistics. He had also been a part of designing the hub in Frankfort, Germany, and in China. He explained to her that their long term plans didn't include a hub in Kazakhstan or Russia but said he would be glad to go to Almaty and consult them on how they could prepare and get ready to start an airfreight business of their own and what it would require to have more FedEx stops at their airport. As I mentioned there were maybe a few stops a week, but there wasn't enough profit in it to make any more at that time. Sofia said that she would be in touch with the airport authorities and see if they could use Josh's services, and the process began to make this happen.

Arman and I made another trip to Houston to introduce Sofia to Frank, and we stayed two nights instead of one. Sofia had never seen interstate systems like she saw on the way to Houston with quadruple layer overpasses. Even the trucks were larger than she was accustomed to. Although she had been all over Russia, Europe, Asia, and China nothing compared to the good ole USA. When we met with Frank at his office along with James about 10:00 a.m., he seemed very sleepy again and ready for the workday to be finished. He was highly impressed with Sofia as they discussed the origins of the Russian oil business with the US, and they were familiar with the diplomats who had brought about the relationship. This was during the Gorbachev era, and Frank had actually been on flights on Soviet military jets from Moscow to Siberia with him checking out newly drilled oil wells. Both Sofia and Frank proved their credibility to each other, and we adjourned the meeting with high hopes and decided to move forward. James chauffeured us around Houston and to the coast to see the shipyards. The next morning we headed back to Memphis and Sofia went back to Almaty believing her visit had been constructive.

When we arrived in Memphis, I received an email from the manager of the Hard Rock Café who I had met in Moscow. He had met a piano player, Dennis, who did a gig there and played a lot of rockabilly, and his idol was Jerry Lee Lewis. He was gaining popularity In Russia and had performed at a recent G2 summit and had also been an opening act for Jerry Lee ten years earlier in Canada. He asked if this may be something we had in mind. It certainly was! Beyond a shadow of a doubt. He gave me Dennis's manager's phone number, and Arman gave her a call, since she didn't speak English. She sent videos of performances, and he was incredible, and we decided to make something happen.

Once again, I called my faithful partner, Paul. He has been promoting an annual hot wings festival in Memphis for the past fifteen years. All of the proceeds go to Ronald McDonald House, and last year they raised nearly $30,000 dollars. Paul has brought in top national musical acts through the years along with the best of the local scene. I sent Paul some of his music, and Paul was more than ready to give him a slot at the festival. This pianist was extremely talented, and Jerry Lee even admitted that he was as fast as he had been in his younger days. We started making plans to get Dennis and his manager over here.

Now, it was February 2011 and time to get back to Almaty and meet the Russian supplier of jet fuel. James had asked his son, Scott, to come along to take notes and help us keep focus. He was a Christian clinical psychologist and had his own practice in east Texas. Arman and I had met him in Houston earlier and were glad to have him on board, since he had been working with James part-time keeping his business ventures organized and was full of fun, like his dad. Scott mentioned to me that he was concerned about Jimmy. He said that his dad had been paying his expenses and had sent him to China several times to work on projects with David, our Chinese partner, who owned restaurants in Memphis. He said that Jerry had run up quite a tab on his last trip in China, and David's brother had also spent money on him.

Jimmy was retired air force and had been in aircraft sales internationally and was full of eye-popping stories. I mentioned that I had met him at church, and he always had a Bible verse to share and would email us parts of his daily devotionals that he thought would encourage us. His daughter, who went to church with us, told me one time that there were some Memphis businessmen that were upset with him. I asked Jimmy about it, and he got me on the phone with a friend of his who convinced me that whatever had happened wasn't his fault. We discussed this with James and decided that he was trustworthy. Scott was wanting us to do our homework before we jumped into this venture with both feet, and he remained suspicious.

Talgat met with us when we arrived and brought one of the players in the ongoing oil deal with Russia and the DOD. He was from Kyrgyzstan and would explain more about the corruption and why Russia wanted to open the upcoming bid to other brokers. Talgat told us before he arrived that he was former KGB and still involved in their current intelligence community and said not to give him any personal details or not to reveal our contact with the DOD. He said that he had known him for many years but he still might try to cut us out of the deal if possible. I noticed his obvious bloodshot eyes, and he resembled the hunchback of Notre Dame. (I was afraid to ask him who he thought I looked like!) We went out to dinner with them at one of Talgat's favorite shish kabob establishments and met in a quiet private room. We had two vodka toasts and this fellow kept pouring himself drinks and offering it to us, and we refused. He seemed to be getting a buzz going and asked us several times who our contact with the DOD was. We told him that we were working through our legal team and weren't able to tell him.

We woke up the next morning and prayed together about our meeting. Then we met this man and his partner along with Talgat and Sofia in a conference room at the Kazakhstan hotel. His partner was with the Russian company who had been supplying jet fuel through the supposedly crooked American broker to the DOD. It was about 10:00 a.m., which was turning out to be the usual time meetings started in Almaty. First out came the vodka and shot glasses for everyone, along with breakfast. We had two toasts, one for each side. James, who is one of the funniest people that I have ever met, looked over at me slyly in the seriousness of the business at hand. He turned his head where our Russian friends couldn't notice and looked at me with his eyes crossed and his tongue sticking out the side of his mouth. The fellow we were with the night before kept offering us shots, as well as pouring more for himself. The executive from the oil company didn't drink after the toasts and was sober and congenial but strictly business.

Sofia began drawing diagrams on a large dry erase board, and the oil man began mapping out the plan with Talgat interpreting. One thing that was a little suspicious was their plan for transporting the jet fuel from the Kazakh border to our Begran air force base. In the specs we had received from the DOD, our part of the deal was finished when the product reached the border. This guy suggested that if we could arrange a contractor to deliver the product from the border to the base that he would include extra fuel for us to sell privately in Afghanistan (what?). We told him that we had no say-so about that, but we would check it out further, just to get him to back off because we had no intention of participating in such a deal and getting killed or going to Guantanamo Bay. After a long stressful morning, we told them that we would be ready for the spring bidding process. Their oil refinery partner said that he was certain that he could get the contract on his side of the deal, or at worst, get us part of it in case Russia decided to use multiple brokers.

James and Scott hung around for a couple of days, and we showed Scott around Almaty. We didn't stay in my apartment during their visit but in another apartment building and when they left, Talgat moved me again to another place. He said he didn't want the oil man's partner to know where I was because he would continue to try to find out more about our business (and Lord knows what else).

The day before heading back to Memphis, Talgat took me snow skiing. The Asian winter games were taking place, and we weren't able to go to the main ski resorts, so he took me to this anti-quated place that had been a former Soviet vacation spot, and we were the only skiers at the slope. This property was currently hous-ing security for the winter games who they had brought in from all over Kazakhstan, and most were very poor having never been away from their hometowns. About ten of them saw us driving past and hurried over to watch us ski. The lift was nothing more than a long water skiing rope with a grip on the end, and Talgat gave me no instructions, so I grabbed hold and started slowly moving up the slope. I was holding on for dear life and went about twenty yards before my hands slipped, and I fell backward, landing on my tailbone. I had experienced that injury before, and it was extremely painful, but I sucked it up and grabbed hold again when another rope passed by. The Kazakh policemen seemed very concerned and made it up the hill to help me and took a picture of us, and Talgat let one of them put on his skis. The slope was solid ice, and I made it down by skiing about fifteen yards at a time and falling down. I had been on skis one time before and partially separated my shoul-der. This time I made it down the slope once and was hurting too bad to try it again.

Talgat wanted to take me back to a friend who he gave the title of 'healer" who had treated me after I had sprained my ankle on a previous visit. I knew it wasn't broken but Talgat insisted I go see this guy and the "healer" proceeded to squeeze my ankle like he was try-ing to draw the swelling out of the bottom of my foot. I have pretty high pain tolerance, but this was awful, and I ended up going back to him two more times because I thought I had to for the sake of doing business with Talgat. By the end of the week, my ankle was well (which it would have been anyway), but then he noticed my knee was swollen from a past surgery. He squeezed the swelling out of that too, and Talgat referred to these as my torture sessions. I told him that I wasn't about to let this guy squeeze the fool out of my butt, and I left for home the next day, struggling to stay seated on the flight.

On the way to the airport, Sofia told me she had something very serious to tell me to relay immediately to James. She said with Talgat translating, "I want you to tell James that we expect him to pay all of our expenses on any trips that we have to take involving this deal." (Great!)

I said, "All of us on our side pay our own expenses on any deal and settle up when, and if, we are paid a commission."

She seemed to be angry, almost threatening, and yelled, "I am very serious!"

I composed myself and told her, "I will talk to James and get him in touch with you.' This was the first time I was fearful about working with them and was ready to get the heck out of Almaty."

James was very unwilling to pay their expenses, and thankfully Sofia didn't confront us with this issue again. Jimmy kept us updated on the bidding process by forwarding our emails from his cousin "Armando."

With the boxing deal, everything seemed to be set on our side with the US Olympic Committee. Arman had been in touch with Talgat and Mikel, and they promised they were making progress on their end. It was getting closer and closer to the Olympic games, and we were getting nervous. Paul's hot wing festival was in the middle of April, and the visas for the pianist and his manager were in the works.

Arman was encouraging Natalie and Reid to spend part of the summer in Russia learning the language and was very adamant about this. Anna and I told him that this was their decision, but in Uzbekistan things were much different and parents usually choose their children's careers and marriage partners. Arman married a lady from Russia, which created quite a stir in his family with his sister and other family members refusing to ever speak to her. His daughter left for Spain when he fled Uzbekistan and ended up marrying a young Spanish man. His wife was able to remain in Uzbekistan because she was a medical doctor on Embassy Row (it's complicated). Anna and I brought his daughter to Memphis from Spain when he hadn't seen her in several years, and it was quite a happy time, to say the least. Arman was a very soft-spoken, handsome, charming man a little younger than myself and had a powerful way of persuasion. Still, these were our kids, and we made it known to him that it was their choice. They both chose to go (of course) and were very excited about it.

They would stay with the family who hosted Natalie and myself. Natalie had become friends with their daughter who had come to our training program. Their dad, Albert, who she met on a previous trip was a doctor who would treat Reid. He had struggled with scoliosis since high school and had to quit running track because of it, and it was starting to impact his activities of daily living. He had received various treatments here which didn't have any lasting effects.

CHAPTER 9

One Step Forward, Three Steps Back

*A*s we were getting closer to the bid date for the jet fuel project, Jimmy headed to DC to meet with his cousin's law firm, which was enormous, with offices all over the country based in Memphis. The next day we definitely received the biggest shock of our lives. James had called Jimmy's apartment to settle up on some of his rent, and the manager casually mentioned that he had just seen Jimmy. James immediately called Jimmy, and he told him that he was at the lawyer's office in DC waiting for the Pentagon to send over some documents.

Arman and I got in the car and drove over to Jimmy's place, and I was very nervous and afraid of what we might encounter. I had a permit to carry and brought my pistol along just in case. When we rolled up, Arman insisted that I leave the gun in the car. He grinned and said, "Jimmy is seventy-something years old, and we can handle him if he gets crazy on us." We walked up to the office door, and it was an extended stay hotel, and we asked if they would ring his room because we didn't want to call from our mobiles.

I called and Jimmy answered. I told him calmly, "Come down and talk to us." We met in the entry and I asked him, "What is going on? James just spoke with you and you told him you were in DC." Jimmy was silent. I tried to be cool and asked him, tongue in cheek, "Is this part of your secret dealings with Armando?" Then I asked him, "Will you meet us in the morning and get on the phone with James?"

He very sharply answered, "Since you don't trust me anymore, I'm out of the deal."

I was thinking, "How could we have been such fools and trusted him like this." "Armando's" law firm in Memphis had helped me with a legal matter a few months earlier. The lawyer was a labor law attorney, who I discovered was one of the founders with Jimmy's cousin. I called him and asked him if he knew Jimmy and if his cousin was working on our project. He told me that his partner didn't have a cousin named Jimmy and was eighty-eight years old, relaxing and doing art projects. We discussed what was going on, and I forwarded him all of Jimmy's emails. Jimmy had done such a good job of covering his tracks that there was no proof of him impersonating the senator, which would have been a criminal act. He was also dating a federal Judge in Memphis and was conning her also. We had been out to dinner with them several times, and she seemed to adore him. The attorney told me he would inform her and not to reach out to her. Most of the con artists that I had known in the past were junkies and could talk you into loaning them money, but Jimmy was a master!

We called Frank, our financial partner in Houston, and it almost ruined our reputation with him because he had already secured the financing for the deal and was very upset. Because of his friendship with James and all the time he had invested, he contacted an army general friend of his that had strong contacts with the DOD, but it was too late for him to even consider getting the bid in. Now we had to contact Sofia and we told her there was a delay, and she didn't freak out like we surely imagined she would. Come to find out the Chinese deals that James had been working on with David had also been with the help of "Armando" and all of us were devastated.

Soon afterward another disappointment slapped us in the face. The Kazakh boxers wouldn't have everything organized in time to have the matches before the Olympics, and then another setback came. Sofia had set up a conference call with the airport authority in Almaty and arranged a Skype meeting. Josh, my FedEx contact, had drawn up a proposal with specific details of our hopeful consulting opportunity. We had a separate contract with him ready to go paying us a very generous percentage of his hourly fee. Josh and I got on the call with Sofia and the airport officials, and the first thing one of the officials said in perfectly good English was, "Josh, I am so happy that you can bring FedEx to Almaty." Silence! I was so embarrassed and upset, and then Josh proceeded to tell them about what we had discussed with Sofia, but evidently she had told them that they would be on the call with FedEx who was ready to start making plans for the new hub. Wow! After that, I ducked my head every time I saw Josh at Kiwanis, but he wasn't too worried about it and said that type thing was common in international business (wish someone had enlightened me two years ago).

After that string of disasters, we decided that would be the end of our dealings with Kazakhstan. My Danish friend Carston had warned me that this was the norm when dealing with them, although I met some very nice Kazakhs who became friends on my visits, and I am sure that is not the case with all of them. We just got involved with the wrong ones and weren't willing to take any more chances (ever again). I was about ready to throw in the towel, and once again Anna and Arman told me not to give up. The Russian pianist was coming soon, and we were working on a number of other projects which were still alive, so against my better business judgment, I decided to carry on.

We chose to focus our attention on the Russian opportunities that were popping up. Arman's aunt and uncle lived in DC and his aunt had been the first ambassador from Uzbekistan to the US. She was encouraging him to come spend a few days with her and meet the Russian Ambassador. Arman had a friend, Nick, from Russia that was coming to DC soon, so he scheduled the visit with his aunt at the same time. This fellow was Molotov's grandson and was an advisor to the Kremlin. He was one of Arman's best friends from their Moscow State and Communist Party days, and his grandfather was Stalin's famous hitman (Molotov cocktail named after him). Arman had met the grandfather several times, forty years earlier, and Nick, along with others, had supposedly helped him escape to this country. I still don't fully understand how this happened because Arman was reluctant to tell the story. Nick seemed anxious to offer his backing of our business ventures with Russia, which, in our eyes, painted another positive picture.

Anna and I agreed to move forward with high hopes and bought Arman a round trip ticket to DC. He stayed with his aunt and uncle and they were able to introduce him to the Russian Ambassador who arranged a meeting with the head of the Russian Cultural Center, Yogi. He was in charge of building and improving relationships with other countries through culture, and Anna was very excited because her favorite part of our efforts had been the cultural exchange projects. She really enjoyed being in Moscow and was becoming to be a dedicated student of Russian history and their language. Yogi had begun to open Russian Cultural Centers in several American cities and was open to the possibility of Memphis being the next. Arman met with his friend Nick and they discussed ways to connect businessmen from our countries, mainly in the oil business, and when he returned my confidence in our ventures came back full force.

It was time for the Russian Jerry Lee Lewis to arrive and we picked them up and took them to our apartment that we had leased for the training classes. We went out for dinner and didn't celebrate with traditional vodka toasts because Dennis was a serious alcoholic in recovery. His manager actually kept twenty-four-hour watch over him in Memphis and instructed us to never leave him alone because his drinking had ruined quite a few lucrative opportunities in Russia.

Along with the hot wings festival, Paul had booked two gigs for him on Beale Street, one at BB Kings and one at the Blues City Café across the street. Anna had arranged for someone to tape the shows and there was also a songwriter in town who had watched YouTube videos of his performances. If things worked out, he wanted to write a song for Dennis and create a music video that we could market here and in Russia.

The hot wings festival was the upcoming Saturday and Paul had him on the schedule. We had one kink because Dennis didn't bring his bass player and drummer, so we were forced to hire them from a local act. When he began to play it was as if the entire several block festival headed towards him and I think it's safe to say that not many had heard anyone play rock in roll piano like that. He certainly was the Jerry Lee of old, and after the festival, he was invited to play at a private party in a large warehouse nearby. The songwriter and cameraman that were with us were truly impressed and were excited about moving forward with the video.

They met with Dennis the next day and wrote a song which was a really cool story about a Russian young man who met a pretty Memphis lady on the banks of the Mississippi River. Monday we rented time at Sun Studio where Jerry Lee, Elvis, and others had recorded and brought back the bass player and drummer. Over the next couple of days, we returned to the warehouse where Dennis had played, shot a couple of scenes on the river, and created a music video. The warehouse had been decorated with old Memphis memorabilia and was the perfect setting. The video was done very professionally and when it was edited and ready to go it cost about $4,000 and Dennis's manager agreed to pay part of the cost.

On Dennis's final evening with us, he played a set at BB Kings and then finished the night at the club across the street. The house bands played with him and were fascinated, and crowds packed both places after he began to play with each club opening the windows and folks gathering outside. These two gigs didn't pay anything, but we hoped it would be a very significant jumpstart for him in Memphis and get him recognition from tourists who come here from all over the world.

Paul rewarded him handsomely for the festival, but we ended up paying for the bass player and drummer, studio, and video production, which meant his stay cost us about $3,000 dollars out of pocket (ouch!). It was time to market the song and video and we wrestled with Dennis's manager about royalties with her believing that Dennis should make the overwhelming majority of the money. In her view, the songwriter shouldn't make hardly anything, but that wasn't quite the way the music business works in the west. The music video turned out really well, and we thought for sure that it would be a success, but in the upcoming weeks his manager never agreed for anyone to make any money except for them. We tried as best as we could but never reached an agreement. Once again, another deal bit the dust.

Again, I was discouraged and having second thoughts about moving forward, but Anna and Arman were unwaveringly full-steam-ahead and somehow persuaded me that the next venture would work. They had been in touch with Yogi, the Russian cultural minister and were convinced that a cultural center in Memphis would attract business contacts. Anna also believed strongly that this would bring us back to our original purpose of leading people to Christ through business and culture and was elated about the possibilities.

The next step was for Anna and Arman to fly to DC and meet the Russian Ambassador and Yogi and they also had meetings scheduled with our US trade representatives with Russia. She had met with our city officials including both mayors and the head of our Memphis Chamber of Commerce and they all gave their support in bringing the center to Memphis. Anna had built relationships with Rhodes College and the University of Memphis Russian professors who looked forward to and committed to working with us. Anna and Arman stayed at a hotel located on the property of the center in DC. It was very beautiful and full of Russian art, which fascinated Anna. The officials at the Russian Embassy agreed with Yogi that Memphis would be the host city for their next cultural center, and we started making plans for Yogi and his wife to visit. There was preparatory work to be done including finding a location for the center for Yogi to approve and arranging a welcoming committee consisting of local government officials and professors.

Natalie and Reid were on summer break from college and it was time for their visit to Moscow where they had Russian language and cultural classes scheduled. Reid was treated by Albert for his scoliosis with a combination of physical therapy, acupuncture, electrical stimulation and other procedures not common in the US such as the mountain air-breathing process that Albert had patented—and leeches! They also were to engage in some upscale private club social life, and their hosts took very good care of them. Reid's back was definitely better when he returned and it was a turning point in his constant battle with continuous pain.

He had one surprise for us when he said, "Dad, after associating with the Russian young people, I have made a final decision. I don't want to do business with Russians! I discovered that, in general, they don't like Americans." (Yep, he sure did.) Albert's daughter warned them several times to not let anyone except her friends hear them speaking in English, while in the private expensive clubs. I never pursued him to engage in business opportunities with them again, to Arman's disappointment, although Reid still loves and appreciates Albert and his family.

Reid was to return one more time over Christmas break for treatment with Albert but decided that he would switch his language major to Spanish. He had worked for landscaping crews during summer breaks and really enjoyed being around the Mexican workers. Natalie enjoyed her time there but was homesick and thrilled to be back and see her future fiance, Joe.

I was spending more time with our homecare agency getting it ready to sell. We were hoping to sell it for around $1,000,000 and I began to get our financials in order to present to future buyers. Our gross sales had slipped to about $1,800,000 from $2,000,000 the previous year and focusing on the Russian ventures didn't help, along with the downturn in the economy. I had lost my zeal to take it to the next level, and it was becoming more obvious that it was time to sell. My office manager and her husband made us a good offer and we wouldn't have to pay a broker and saved at least 10 percent. They were sharp business people, both coming from families that were business owners, but we would need to finance the sale and they would have to grow the business or keep it at the current level to be able to pay us. We agreed on a substantial down payment and a monthly note that would more than cover our expenses. We made the sale for an amount close to our goal and they succeeded over the next five or six years and made timely payments.

CHAPTER 10

>+*+<

The Russians Are Coming

*Y*ogi and his wife paid us a visit, and we met with a group of interested parties that would become our board of directors. We found a vacancy in the art district on South Main which would be the home of the Memphis Russian Cultural Central for the next two years. Anna, Arman, and myself spent time with Russian professors and with a realtor friend of mine because Yogi had expressed interest in opening a small hotel near the cultural center for Russian diplomats and tourists to reside when they visited. He was also impressed with the robust housing and business development downtown and on Mud Island and promised he knew Russian investors who would be interested. My realtor friend, Larry, was also in the process of developing a high-end women's retreat in the Ozarks with a bluegrass and folk music theme. Many people from Memphis had weekend and retirement cabins there, and Yogi wanted to hear more about it and possibly visit the mountains on his next trip. I was really excited for Anna who was stepping further into her element, and once again my spirits were up.

This extremely important phase for us was materializing, but my major concern was the $1,500 a month rent payment. Anna and Arman assured me that Yogi's center in DC would be footing the bill, and we spent time designing the center which included building shelves, a stage, and adding flooring. We also purchased a large screen TV for presentations and Russian movies, along with a sound system. We painted the room based on the color scheme of the center in DC and Yogi sent us posters to put in the windows and on the walls and a Russian flag to hang beside an American flag outside.

Within a month, it was ready for the grand opening celebration in January 2012. Both our city and county mayors would be part of the ribbon-cutting along with a bipartisan group of local and state politicians and our US Congressman, Steve Cohen. The president of Rhodes College and Congressman Cohen would speak with Anna giving a summary of our plans for the center. Yogi would explain the overall purpose and goal of the effort, with Arman interpreting, and the priest from the local Orthodox church would be there to bless the effort and lead us in prayer.

The ceremony exceeded our expectations with a celebratory atmosphere. One of our local news channels was present, and the event was on air that evening with the press from Russia and our local media covering the event with cameras flashing. We had an overflow crowd, standing room only, spilling out onto the sidewalk, and we even had a Russian bodyguard who was a bouncer for several clubs downtown.

Yogi was only in town for a few days and he and his wife opted to stay at a ritzy hotel downtown instead of our guest apartment. He had promised our realtor friend that they would look at some investment properties the next day, but when Larry skipped church Sunday morning and arrived to pick them up, Yogi's wife said she didn't feel well, and they didn't make it, which was disappointing, but he assured our partner he would be back with investors.

We were to meet many of the Russian locals in the months to come, most of which were ladies who had married Memphis men they had met online. As word got out, we soon met Russian scientists doing research at St. Jude and different institutes in Memphis. One was an elderly gentleman whose lifelong project was cancer research, and he had created a new type of medicine that was having great results in the test lab.

The first month Yogi promised a number of books to begin a Russian Library, and right off the bat Arman started offering Russian language classes and had ten students in the beginning. Anna started hosting Russian movie nights, and several of the ladies from the former Soviet Union, including Ukraine, began to bring and fill the building with artwork, pottery, and artifacts. Every time there was a Russian holiday, Anna would invite their community to come and celebrate. Their holiday for the end of WW2 was V-E day or Victory in Europe day which was one that our countries could share. She invited sons of veterans like myself and located several whose dads had fought for the other side and this resulted in arm wrestling contests and of course vodka shot contests (they won). One of Anna's friends taught belly dancing lessons and many of the ladies participated, including her. There was only one restaurant in town that served Russian cuisine, and they invited the ladies to come dressed in traditional costumes and perform for special events. The belly dancing and language classes went on for almost three years and grew considerably every Tuesday night.

In the spring, Trolley Night takes place in the Art District on South Main, and the cultural center was in the very center of the activities. On Trolley Night, the last Friday of every month, every shop was displaying their art and offering wine and cheese, so our center would offer (you guessed it) vodka shots and a Russian dish like Piroshki which is similar to an Italian Calzone, or Borscht which is beet soup. Anna would usually find musicians from the local Russian students who would volunteer to perform, and one of which was a violinist who played often and would sometimes bring an orchestra with her. Anna would always have local artists to display and sell their work with Arman there to shed light on the culture and with me outside hawking prospects.

But unfortunately, we discovered as time went on that the center wasn't making any money, so I decided to get a real estate license in anticipation of Yogi's promised investors. I wanted to do this in case I started selling, so I could get a legal commission and also earn extra income in other real estate markets. Arman had been in touch with Yogi, and he had found several investors interested in the Ozark resort, and there was a program going on at the time rewarding foreigners, with a visa for a family member, if they invested a certain amount in an American business. He said he had many friends that would like for their children to come here for educational purposes, and that would be an excellent opportunity.

My realtor friend, Larry, suggested Arman and I come over to the prospective site and check it out and meet his Arkansas partners. Anna, Natalie, Reid and I had been to the area many times camping, and it was one of our favorite places. They planned a large cookout and bonfire on the White River for Arman and knew that when he saw the property, he would be excited to get the word out. When it was time to go, Arman said at the last minute that he couldn't make the trip, and our associates were confused and disappointed. Anna and I showed up without him, and we all had a big-time anyway.

I received a license after a grueling study and test for the exam (too old for that) and started working with Larry. The first house that I showed sold, but I was working mostly on commercial property, and it was very slow in those days in Memphis. Larry suggested I come and work out of his Ozark office on weekends and sell land and cabins, and Anna and I agreed and believed it would give us a chance to make money until the center took off.

We were doing okay until Yogi stopped paying the rent and expenses which he abruptly halted after the fourth month. I was visibly irritated, but Arman would always say the check was on the way with Anna remaining hopeful. She was speaking to women's groups and gaining popularity with local and national politicians and making contact with prominent Memphians. She was invited to Moscow to a meeting with our Ambassador to Russia to discuss foreign relations and to St Petersburg to organize student exchanges with Russia.

Anna was really shining and coming into her own as an ambassador for Memphis and Tennessee. She could walk in, usually without an appointment, and see both of our mayors and get their approval for anything she wanted to do. She was becoming a polished public speaker, prettier and happier than ever, and we were so proud of her, and it made me feel like a big shot just being seen with her.

Reid went to Moscow in the winter of 2012 for his final round of spinal treatments. He returned without pain, for the most part, and continues to do the exercises Albert prescribed to strengthen weak areas of his back, and to him, we are eternally grateful. Reid is able to run and play basketball again and has resumed comfortably his normal routines.

Once again when I was having negative thoughts about our Russian escapades, another ray of hope broke through my despair. In the spring of 2013, I was attending a Chamber of Commerce one-on-one luncheon with selling real estate in mind. The chamber would place you together for networking purposes with other members, and the fellow I met with worked with a local wind energy company. They designed windmills that powered batteries on electric automobiles and boats and were working on a contract with an electric car manufacturer. I asked him, "Are you involved with anything internationally?"

He said, "No, but we are open to the possibility."

I told him, "I have contacts in Russia. Would you find out if your owner has any interest?" He was happy to do so, and we left the meeting pleased that the Chamber had brought us together.

Arman called Yogi and told him about this opportunity, and come to find out, the former Soviet country of Tatarstan had in the works the building of a smart city with only electric cars allowed. They emailed us information, and the wind energy company was very open to having windmills charge car batteries in this city, and hopefully, the electric cars from their new partner. I scheduled a meeting with this local company, and we walked away from the meeting with all parties excited and confident about moving forward.

Yogi's associate with Tatarstan, George, lived temporarily in DC and was on assignment in the US as a trade representative from Russia. In about two weeks we were scheduled to have an important conference at the University of Memphis law school about trade and other issues with Russia. One major hindrance of trade between our countries was the human rights violations which caused us great concern. Yogi was to speak and answer questions, and George would also attend. The vice president of the school was from Russia but had been here for years and was an American citizen and a frequent visitor at the center. He had put this conference together with us in mind.

Arman had asked George if they were looking for any other products that we might supply along with the windmills, and George told him that their oil business was extensive, and they imported a great deal of their supplies, especially cold weather safety gear. A friend of mine from high school, Johnny, worked for a large safety supply company in Texas. I spoke with him and his company was furnishing cold-weather gear for oil companies drilling in the Dakotas. He was happy to give us a quote, and although his company wasn't doing business internationally, they were very open to the idea. He agreed to come to the conference and set up a display of his products and sent us a price list which Arman translated into Russian.

Also attending the conference would be faculty from the law school, presidents of the Memphis and Tennessee Chambers, a state senator, and the attorney who was the chairman of our cultural center's board of directors. Yogi and George, along with their wives, and the windmill company owner and the electric car manufacturer would participate. On the day of the conference, the car manufacturer brought an electric car and displayed it on Front Street in front of the school, and the windmill company brought one of their portable windmills and placed it by the car for a demonstration. Johnny set up his display in the conference room which featured oil-resistant, head to toe, cold weather protection. It was an interesting meeting with the law professor, along with Anna and Yogi, addressing the audience with the professor's topic being how to bring about more trade and interaction between our countries. Then Anna emphasized how that was the purpose of our center, and then Yuri emphasized how it was the intent of the Russian government to work out obvious problems with human rights issues. Next, we went around the table with Johnny, the car manufacturer, and the wind company owner promoting their products. In the end, we agreed to come together again to propose solutions.

The next day George met with Arman and myself and looked at some businesses that I had listed for sale. These businesses would meet the requirements for acquiring visas if purchased by Russians, and George appeared to have an interest. Yogi wanted to visit Graceland, and he was very impressed, and I went along with him and Arman and also really enjoyed it. I had grown up about two miles down the road and never took the tour because we all seem to take it for granted around here. Anna took Yogi's wife shopping for clothes for their grandchildren which are in abundant supply here, unlike Russia, and reasonably priced, and then we all met for dinner.

George said that Johnny's prices were in the ballpark and was impressed with the windmill and electric car, and then he brought up something that popped my bubble. He said that near Tatarstan was a huge vacant former Soviet air force base designed for large cargo planes. He said that if we could just get him a meeting with Fred Smith that he would have no trouble pushing through our deals (here we go again, unbelievable). We had that question answered when dealing with Kazakhstan and knew emphatically that FedEx had no plans for a hub anywhere in the former Soviet Union. I realized that this was dead in the water right then and assumed Arman had relayed that news, but I told him I would check with my contacts at FedEx (why did I think this would be easy?).

I continued to go to the Ozarks on weekends and rented a room in a cabin that belonged to Larry's family. It was the perfect spot for me and was a break from the fiery darts that were coming at me from our international trials and tribulations. It was on the White River, and when I would get to the foothills of the mountains all the worries of the world would seem to lift right off of me. I sold a little real estate and had a lot of listings, but most places were overpriced, and it was the worst possible time I could have entered the market (was I blind to that obvious fact also?)

I would get back to Memphis usually too late to go to church on Sundays, and Anna wasn't going as often, both of us consumed with other pursuits. I was still praying and having a morning devotion but was starting to miss being in ministry with a community of believers and the fellowship that came with folks truly concerned for each other. Anna and I continued to believe that we were doing the right thing with the cultural center, even though doubts were creeping in and taking up too much space in my head. In the last two years, we hadn't made a dime and were steadily pouring money into it, especially our investment in Arman. He was teaching ESL classes on Saturday and getting the majority of the tuition, and I was wondering if I had misread his apparently sharp business skills. I was also going after other international commodity deals with folks that I met on my own who had no former business dealings with Arman.

I had made many contacts and discovered that I wasn't the only one pursuing these deals. I met someone from Peru at Starbucks who had been working on different projects with China and introduced him to my friend David, and we tried to make things happen. All of those time-consuming endeavors just fell apart sooner or later, but we didn't want to give up because of the money and effort we were putting into it. I was finally getting it through my thick skull that these deals were all long shots and that to be involved you had to be wealthy enough not to miss losing a few thousand dollars (or more). Anna and I were definitely missing it, having invested much more than we were making and were starting to feel it.

There was one more target in my sights at making something happen with commodities through my friend Carsten, from Denmark. Carsten, James, and I would be meeting with Frank in Houston, who wasn't holding the jet fuel deal against us, and a timber mill owner who was a friend of James. Carsten was representing the largest oil and energy company in Russia who was looking for a certain kind of wood chip used for fuel to heat homes in Russia. Two of Carstens's friends from Rotterdam would be there to network and explore ways to do business. Rotterdam is a major shipping port for Europe and these guys owned a shipyard there, and it would be a possible shipping connection between Houston and that part of the world. The timber mill was about one hundred miles from Houston, and the deal might have worked, but after spending time figuring out how to get the product from the mill to the Houston shipyards, the cost would be too much for us to make any money (another non-profitable trip to Houston).

Anna was still having the time of her life making contacts and expressing herself in new fulfilling ways. I was thinking about telling her that she needed to get a part-time job, but she was still convinced that something good was going to happen, so I refrained. Arman wasn't discouraged at all and kept reminding me that all it would take was one big break, and we would easily make back our money. Anna continued to have more and more projects at the center, and the Trolley Nights were bringing in lots of tourists and visitors. She was able to have nice Russian art pieces brought in from around the country, on consignment, which she expected to sell and make a commission.

I wasn't exactly panicking about our finances and thought the real estate business would pick up and bring in more than enough, and I continued my weekend trek to Arkansas. I began taking our fourteen-year-old dachshund, Bruiser, with me, and we would hop in the jeep and drive around on the back roads late every afternoon when I got off. We met some really nice, laid-back people, and I found myself enjoying a little too much wine on the porch at night with neighbors. Bruiser became a hit with the locals mainly because of his addiction to licking frogs (he sure was). He would lick them and foam at the mouth and would appear to be tripping. He would collect them and hide them under the brush along the creek beds, and they would be gathered there, playing dead. He had a lifelong addiction and never kicked the habit, and we never discouraged him or held an intervention. Anna came over and spent a few weekends and one time brought Arman with her, but her great love for the outdoors had been overshadowed and wasn't a priority. When we were first married, it was her primary goal to get back to the mountains to live, and I was hoping she would come more often just to clear her head.

Back in Memphis on Mondays, I would hit the pavement making phone calls looking for commercial listings and buyers. Quite a few of the commercial developers moved to Nashville in the middle of the crash from 2010–2013 because those counties didn't seem to be affected, but Memphis was hit hard and super slow recovering.

Anna had brought on another board member for the center that Yogi had suggested. He had family roots in Russia and had written a biography about the first female Russian fighter pilot which was an interesting read filled with history lessons unknown to most Americans. He came to Memphis and had a book signing at the cultural center, and quite a few members of the local Russian community bought books as did some of our faithful friends. He worked out a nice commission for us in the hope that we could sell them, but I couldn't give them away to the majority of our friends who were still uninterested and skeptical about Russia. He was a really cool, retired successful businessman and paid a month's rent, for which we were very grateful.

It was 2013, and for the next six months Anna continued to have more speaking engagements sharing about Russian culture and was hoping to reverse the negative view of our society. She was a faithful student of Arman in his language classes and was becoming more and more fluent and was definitely not sharing my pessimism. Finally, I told Anna that I thought we couldn't afford to keep paying Arman and needed to get his car back, but she resisted and was still optimistic that his connections would pay off.

Anna had been invited to St. Petersburg during the summer of 2013 to formally begin a student exchange program between the two nations through Yogi's connections, and he had convinced her that during the fall we would receive a nice administration fee. It came to the point before she left that our bank balance was becoming frightening low. It was finally unmistakably evident to Anna that we had to stop supporting Arman, from strictly a business perspective. He brought the Expedition by the house and seemed to understand, but almost miraculously, within a few days, he was driving another late model car (what?) Anna's trip to St Petersburg was fascinating, being able to experience the history of that beautiful place, and things were lining up for the student exchange, except it wasn't going to happen that fall.

When Anna returned, Arman immediately informed her about a forum in Moscow that would be for Americans under thirty, which Yogi was spearheading and financing. It would be centered around business and government and educate these young people and introduce them to their systems. They were to visit the Kremlin and converse with leaders in the government and then spend time with business executives. They would lodge at one of the finest hotels and be wined (vodka) and dined and treated like royalty, completely at Russia's expense. Arman advised Anna on who would be the best attendees, and they were all hand-picked. One was a state senator, and several were young businessmen, and one was on our US

Congressman Cohen's staff, and one was a law student, along with others from varying backgrounds. Arman sold me on the idea that they would come back with lifelong contacts that would be profitable for us. I asked Arman to set up meetings with each of them upon return to find out what they had learned and how it would help them with their careers and future ventures with us. Anna and Arman made it a point to get their undivided attention and made them aware that this was the purpose of handpicking them for this trip. With the five or six who took the time out of their schedules to get back with us, we didn't get any feedback except that they had a blast partying, but at least Anna and I didn't fork out the money for this bust.

Just as things were getting financially tighter and tighter, the buyers of our franchise paid their balance in one lump sum, and this brought about one of the toughest decisions of our marriage. Our funds would no longer come out of the same bucket because I insisted that we relied on this money and that I was not investing any more into the cultural center, so we split the money into separate private accounts.

The real estate wasn't working either, and I knew business broker friends that I had networked with, and they gave me another idea which was helping people buy and sell businesses. I knew how businesses were supposed to run, learning the hard way, from years of being self-employed. Anna and I had helped young entrepreneurs in the past start businesses with seed money and launch them and help them set up their finances on QuickBooks and assist them for the first year in running their business. I could value a business by looking at the books, if they were in order, and watching the profit margins. I decided to take the exam and went to work for the largest business brokerage firm in the country. This was commission only, but I was confident it was something that I could make work. They had a system that was successful, and I believed that I could follow it and started working in West TN, North Mississippi, and all over Arkansas.

CHAPTER 11

※

Spies in Disguise

*L*ittle did we know that an event was soon to take place that would drastically change our lives forever. Anna and I visited Reid in Knoxville and spent three wonderful relaxing days with him seeing the sights and sounds of that quaint Tennessee town and enjoying his company. On the ride back, about one hundred miles from Nashville, Anna's phone rang, and it was an FBI agent in Knoxville who assumed we were still there. Two agents had come to visit us in Memphis earlier that morning and Natalie opened the door when they knocked. They introduced themselves as being from a government agency, not wanting to alarm her, and wanted to speak with us and seemed to know quite a bit about us. Natalie told them that we were out of town visiting our son. They knew where Reid was, and a local agent had been to his dorm room, but he wasn't there. The agent on the phone told Anna that they had very important news for us and ordered us to stop at their Nashville office on the way home. We didn't have a clue what they wanted and weren't too bothered. When we arrived at the office, four agents met us, and two of them took Anna, and the other two took me, to separate rooms (just like you see on TV). They asked me if I knew Yogi and wanted to let me know that he was a Russian spy and being deported, then they asked about my relationship with him and how long that I had known him. They inquired about Arman and our relationship with him, and I answered every question in great detail. They told me that I would be assigned an agent to work with in Memphis and that I needed to meet with him first thing the next morning. They asked Anna pretty much the same questions, which she informed me on the way home, and she was assigned another agent to meet the next morning at a different location.

On the way back to Memphis, Anna called the attorney who was the chairman of our board of directors, and he told her not to meet with the FBI alone. Arman had been contacted, and Anna and he had the attorney schedule a meeting for them with a criminal defense lawyer. Natalie also got a call to meet an agent in Memphis at another location. I didn't have a problem meeting with them alone, nor did Natalie, and we totally cooperated with them. I told Anna after meeting with the Memphis agent that I believed that Arman was involved, and that I was disassociating myself from him and everything that had anything to do with the Russian Cultural Center.

From this meeting going forward I cannot, as a matter of national security, say anything about any further communication with the FBI, and all that I can say is that this type of investigation is not a sprint but a marathon! After Anna and Arman's meeting with the FBI, they instructed them to shut down the center because they claimed that Yogi had used the center and the gathering in Russia to recruit spies. This story made the national news, and Anna was interviewed on local TV along with several attendees, including the state senator. During his interview, the senator said that he thought we paid for his trip and said that he had no idea the Russian government funded it (really?). Next, they interviewed everyone that we had sent to Moscow and then contacted all of my real estate partners in Arkansas.

I decided that Arman knew what Yogi was up to, but Anna refused to believe it and couldn't fathom how I could take the FBI's word for it. She continued to trust him completely. We couldn't get past this and were far more upset and angry with each other than ever before. My business contacts and personal friends that had worked with Arman and associated with him were very troubled and told me that they trusted Arman because they trusted me, and this was horrible for Anna's and my reputations. Anna said Arman was furious and said that what they saw in him was what they got, and he was totally unapologetic and wanted no part in clearing his name with my associates.

Over the next couple of weeks, it was hard for us to talk about anything. Anna said that her feelings for me were gone, and I asked her if she wanted a divorce, and she nodded yes. There were never harsh words or raised voices between us. It was as if we were agreeing that this was an impossible, irreconcilable situation.

I realized that we had both drifted from the Lord when we couldn't even pray together about it. Wow! We were praying together less and less when I started going to Arkansas, and we had always prayed about our decisions and about what was happening with the cultural center. There had been slowly but surely a loss of focus on what mattered most to us, and as the spiritual leader of our family, I felt like I had dropped the ball by not nurturing our relationship and making it our top priority (still do).

Thanksgiving of 2013 was soon approaching, and I grieved knowing that it would be our last one together as a family, and it was the hardest weekend of my life, thus far. I had told the kids that Anna and I were having a very tough time but hadn't mentioned the divorce. Christmas was next, and it was even more excruciating for me. I asked Anna several times if she was sure we were doing the right thing, and she, very reluctantly, would say that she did. We had been having New Year's Eve parties at our home every year since the kids were small, and some of the same folks and their children had been coming for twenty-five years. We had the party with hardly anybody knowing what we were going through, and it was another gut-wrenching holiday.

The divorce was final in February 2014, and I moved out and kept the place in the Ozarks and used it for a base when working in Arkansas. I rented a small apartment in Midtown and Anna remained in the house on Peabody, and we listed it for sale. We split the rent on all the residences and everything else right down the middle, such as our kids' tuition, and we continued to believe that reconciliation was impossible.

When the center shut down, Anna and Arman went to work for the wind energy company that I had introduced them to with

Anna working in sales and Arman assisting with administrative tasks. Even though the center was officially closed, they continued to have the Russian language classes and still had frequent gatherings with the Russian community. They finally got the group from Tatarstan an appointment with FedEx, but it did not result in a hub for their country. All of the other possibilities with Tatarstan also fell through.

Anna and I had very little contact for the next year and a half, except for taking care of business. After the divorce, I thought I would try online dating, and I was contacted on Facebook by a couple of female friends from the past who had heard the news. One was a woman who I met my first year in college, and she had introduced me to several Christian families and students in the faith groups on campus. She wanted to pay me a visit in Memphis, and when she arrived she still seemed to be on fire for God, except for her views on sex outside of marriage. I quickly found myself giving in (the first night) and I felt terrible the next day and knew it was wrong. She definitely wasn't someone that I was interested in marrying, and that is what she said she was hoping for. Shortly afterward, I had almost exactly the same experience with a former high school friend and ended the relationship abruptly, not wanting to lead her on or hurt her.

I met several ladies for coffee on the dating sites, but none of them looked anything like their pictures, and I only met one that I was interested in taking out again. This one I actually took out for dinner, and she was about ten years younger than me and very attractive. The next morning I was on Facebook and there was a message from another lady that I went to school with. She, Carol, asked me, "Who was the blonde at the table with you? You were so enthralled with her that I couldn't get your attention. I walked by and waved at you a couple of times and decided to leave you alone." We talked for a while, and she told me that she had been divorced for a long time and still recovering from what was a horribly abusive marriage. She let me know on the front end, emphatically, that she wasn't looking for a husband and had done the dating site thing with negative experiences, to say the least. She had met a pastor at a church she was attending who had been in a similar situation and really cared for him, but both were afraid to move forward. Anyway, Carol and I decided that we would be friends and hang out, and we went to Sunday night worship services together every once and a while and attended outdoor concerts at a Memphis Park. We began to pray for each other regularly, and I started spending time alone with God again. She had two kids and two grandkids, and it was seriously as if she rescued me from pursuing harmful things that I knew weren't right which I called the three W's: whiskey, weed and wild women. I never even kissed her, and we agreed from the beginning that we wouldn't go the sexual route. She said numerous times that she believed that Anna and I would get back together, although I told her it would be impossible, and I wasn't praying for Anna or our reconciliation.

I worked as a business broker for about a year and traveled as far east as Nashville and worked all over Arkansas and North Mississippi. I found it very easy to get listings because many were ready to sell their businesses, but not many were making a profit which was the key. I found that many profitable businesses didn't keep good records and couldn't prove their income and cash flow, and I spent too much time reconstructing their books. I had three large businesses listed which should have earned me about $300,000 in commission and spent hours meeting potential buyers and going over financials and introducing them to owners.

Earlier that year when I still had what I thought was plenty of money, I unwisely invested $14,000 in a friend's business which I thought was a sound investment. Within the first five months, he fell behind in payroll taxes and filed for bankruptcy, and I only got back about $1,000 dollars, and the rest is gone forever (that one was hard to shake off).

It was approaching Thanksgiving 2014, and I hadn't made a dime all year. For that holiday, which I was dreading, Natalie's future husband, Joe, invited me to his family dinner, and it was a huge blessing. Between Thanksgiving and Christmas, all three of my big deals fell apart, and one night it dawned on me that I was about to be broke. The next morning my daily devotional said that I was walking through the valley of humility and asked if I could trust God and not panic. Uhhhh, no. I pretty much freaked out and knew that I had to do something else quickly (I was wound up tighter than a coon dog trying to pass a peach seed).

I let my place in the Ozarks and my midtown apartment go and moved into a very small high rise apartment in downtown Memphis with my dog Bruiser. I couldn't find a job making good money that wasn't straight commission, so I started driving for Uber and did that for about three months. It wasn't too terribly bad, but it was humbling when I ran into friends that asked me what the heck I was doing it for. It was a lifesaver, and God provided for me and also let me know that He was the source of my income, and that I wasn't some cool, self-made big-shot.

When Christmas rolled around, Reid was working out of town and came home a week early and celebrated Christmas with Natalie and me. On Christmas Day, I didn't have any family to spend it with, being the first time in thirty-three years that we hadn't spent that day together with Anna's family. My parents had both passed away, and I am an only child. Carol called to wish me a Merry Christmas and invited me to spend it with her mom and all of her family which was very kind of them, and it certainly dulled the pain. I admit that I was starting to have feelings for Carol and thought about her often. She was still very attractive and was so sweet and laid back and had her spiritual life together. She had emotionally supported me through the past year, but I knew it wasn't possible for anything serious to come about in our relationship.

Then something very wonderful transpired, and Joe asked Natalie to marry him (finally). They had been dating for years, and I couldn't have handpicked a better guy for her. Through this, Anna and I started discussing and helping with the wedding plans, and we spoke about our relationship, and she jokingly asked me if I thought I could love her again. I responded wholeheartedly that I thought I could, and that conversation planted the seed in my head that I really wanted her back. We talked about the Lord, and I told her that I was genuinely trying to come back to Him and asked her, "Are you feeling that tug from the Holy Spirit?"

She didn't say yes or no but said, "I don't know how to come back to Him!" From that day forward, I began to ask God to bring us back to Himself and then for us to be reconciled.

After a few months of driving for Uber, I went to work selling commercial telecommunication systems for one of the industry leaders. It provided a decent base salary and very good commission but was a lot of cold calling and door knocking. I worked Monday through Friday 7:00 a.m. to 6:00 p.m. and hated going through the Yellow Pages making one hundred phone calls a day. I started attending a large active church on Sunday mornings and sometimes would go with Carol to the other church on Sunday evenings, but I still wasn't plugged in with a group of good Christian friends and found myself very isolated except for getting together with Natalie, usually once a week for lunch or dinner, and Carol less frequently.

After working such long days, I would simply go home and crash. I had my old dog Bruiser with me, and I would take him to a nearby park every morning and every night. He would be able to wait for me every weekday between 6:30 a.m. and 6:30 p.m. without needing to go outside. I found myself visiting a little downtown neighborhood bar on Friday nights and having a few beers. Saturdays I would go for long walks with Bruiser who became well known by everyone on Main Street, including the homeless. Saturday night I would sit outside with Bruiser, weather permitting, and people-watch and drink wine, usually from one of the patios on Main Street. The weekend drinking was beginning to become a habit. I realized later that the vodka toasts had eased me back into enjoying the buzz of alcohol, and that became my stagnant, unfulfilling life.

CHAPTER 12

※

She Loves Me, She Loves Me Not

I decided that I didn't want to date anybody and wasn't going to try, especially after Anna said we needed to get together more often and discuss Natalie's wedding plans. I asked her a few times if she was open to getting back together, and she would always say that it wasn't the right time. In October 2015, Natalie and Joe and had a beautiful wedding. Anna and I worked together all day preparing and even danced together, and it was really a special time for all of us. I had never seen Natalie so happy, and we were overjoyed to have Joe in the family. It seemed as if Anna and I were practically married and I knew for certain that she was the only one that I wanted. I really began to pray for us to get back together. I found out from Carol that she was seeing her pastor friend again and was hoping to marry him. That was a confirmation to me that I should stop dating and wait for Anna.

After the wedding, Anna wasn't as interested in seeing me as often. I was working the day before Thanksgiving and Christmas Eve, but she invited me to dinner with her family on both of these occasions, and it was so much better than the awful loneliness and separation that I had experienced the year before.

My office was a thirty-minute drive from my apartment downtown and about forty-five minutes back home in the heavy afternoon traffic. A friend of mine had a place near my office and was out of town about three-quarters of the time and asked me to move in. It was only a five-minute drive from work, so I made the move, and the shorter commute was wonderful.

The phone systems weren't selling like I had hoped they would while spending three days a week on the phone and visiting businesses on other days. I covered all of the mid-south and sold quite a few systems, but several of the larger prospects fell through. I had an opportunity to sell all of the Fred's Dollar Stores in the US and a large network of surgery centers, but unfortunately, after the first of the year, these sizable deals went with a competitor. My company decided to put me on straight commission, and I couldn't make a living and was forced to find something else.

I sent resumes everywhere and was really hoping to get back into the assisted living community in sales or management but wasn't successful. My friend that I moved in with owned a promotional product and police supply business, and I went to work for him but struggled to make ends meet. I also sold golf clubs for a local sporting goods store. I was making enough to get by, but it was killing my knees being on my feet all day, and I had a groin injury that exacerbated the knee problems. There were days when I didn't know if I was going to be able to walk to my car when I got off, but it was paying the bills and I certainly couldn't quit.

The wind energy company Anna and Arman were working for went out of business. When they shut down, Anna went to work teaching art lessons at a business where people would come and paint pictures, with Anna's instruction, while drinking wine or their favorite beverage. Anna was again in her element with her artistic talent and was a great teacher with very encouraging and humor filled lessons. She was also able to start spending more and more time with her personal art projects, being a truly gifted artist in many different media forms and also inspired others to discover a talent they might not have known that they had.

Anna's mother had developed cancer, and we were hoping that she would make it through Natalie's wedding, and she did. I was able to stay in touch with Anna's parents during her mom's battle, and her parents continued to keep up with me and loved me. Her mother passed away in the summer of 2016, and they asked me to officiate the memorial service, and it just happened to take place on our wedding anniversary. After the service, I was very emotional and cried (which I do once every ten years or so), and Anna asked me what was wrong with my eyes, and I told her I had been crying about it all being the same day. Anna didn't appear to be very upset about the anniversary part of it, but an event soon took place that let me know she still cared.

I was working one night putting up new golf clubs that had arrived and went to get a drink out of a vending machine. My hand wouldn't work to grab it, and I felt numbness in my forearm and it went limp. Right away, I realized what was going on having taken care of my dad for two years while he was paralyzed on the left side after having a stroke. I was becoming disoriented and told my boss I was going to the emergency room and got in my car (real smart) and proceeded to the nearest hospital. I wasn't sure they would accept my insurance, but I was going to try that one first. I hopped on the interstate which wasn't the right route to the hospital. After arriving and parking in front of what I mistook for the emergency room, I frantically walked around and finally found it. When I told the receptionist I thought I was having a stroke, they took me back immediately, and after about an hour the symptoms started to subside.

I didn't want to scare Natalie, but I decided I needed to let someone know what was going on, and she didn't answer. I left her a message to call me when she had a minute, and I called Anna, and she answered and said she was on the way. I tried to tell her I was getting better, but she insisted she come and bring me something to eat. As soon as I hung up the phone, they informed me that they were going to rush me to their stroke center downtown by ambulance. They only had a couple of hours to give me the special clot-busting medicine, if my symptoms got worse. I called Anna back and told her to hold on because I didn't know if I would be going home or staying. After three days in the hospital, they diagnosed it as a TIA and wanted to insert a loop monitor in my chest to record data to see if the stroke was caused by AFIB. Anna came to pick me up at the hospital and reached over and grabbed my hand and said that she did care about me and held it all the way back to get my car.

From that point on, I fervently prayed, more than ever, for God to bring her back and reconcile our marriage. A few weeks later, she drove me to have the device implanted, and over the next six months, Anna would be my chauffeur to outpatient surgeries. The groin problem got much worse, and I continued to believe it was a muscle problem. I went and had an ultrasound and they found a problem with my bladder. I had struggled with bladder issues for ten years but just thought it was basic old man problems, waking up five or six times a night to go to the bathroom. I assumed that every man my age had to carry an empty Gatorade bottle in the car with him. They discovered that my bladder was almost totally stopped up, and I had surgery within a week. (was rotor-rootored). Anna escorted me to the surgery center and to her house to stay overnight to watch me, but the procedure didn't solve the groin pain issue. They had also discovered a hernia and decided that may be contributing, so Anna drove me to another outpatient surgery and home with her for another overnight stay on the sofa to make sure there were no complications.

Between my surgeries, Anna had her gallbladder removed, and I watched her during the daytime and Natalie at night for a couple of days. She was still a little cold towards me as far as our relationship was concerned, so I decided I needed to start romancing her again after her dad informed me of this age-old technique (duh). I am a very poor romancer, but I started to try and sent her flowers for Valentine's Day, Mother's Day, and birthday with a nice card. On our anniversary, along with flowers, I wrote her the most romantic letter of my life telling her how much I missed her and wanted her back. After she lost the job with the wind energy firm, her dad bought her a house, and I started dropping by and cutting the grass and doing home repairs and painting jobs.

I rode with her one day to visit her dad, who was still grieving his wife terribly, and on the way back Anna asked me if I had told her dad that Arman was trying to get her money. I certainly believed it, but I hadn't said that to Anna's dad and surely didn't tell her that. As it turned out, Anna's dad and brothers had visited her on what amounted to an intervention and they told her, not asked her, to cut off all of her support for and contact with Arman or risk losing the house and her inheritance. Her dad stated very emphatically that Arman was never to come to the house again, and Anna knew he was very serious. Her dad told me about this later, and that he was very upset with Arman and considered him a threat.

I continued to go by Anna's periodically and ride bikes with her. I noticed when I would hug her goodbye it was half-hearted, at best, from her standpoint, and when I would ask her about getting back together, she would say that practically it would be the right thing for our family, but she wasn't there emotionally. I realized that I shouldn't put pressure on her but made it clear that it was the desire of my heart, if her feelings changed. We became good friends again, and it was very easy for us to be around each other, although not romantically from her perspective. It was wonderful to be able to visit with the kids and her together, and Natalie and Reid were thrilled and sincerely wanted us to be married again. Instead of them seeing us separately which took time and planning, we could all go out to eat or visit in our homes together and that was INCREDIBLE!

I went to work part-time to supplement the golf club sales doing financials for a lady who was recently widowed. She was over-whelmed with her husband's business which was suddenly placed upon her and was struggling to keep it afloat. This was perfect for me, and I was hoping that it would grow into something full time. My groin pain was getting much worse, but I wasn't able to quit the golf sales because I needed the money. I went ahead and took early social security and that combined with the part-time jobs allowed me to save some money and relax a bit.

It was July of 2017, and Anna informed me that she had accepted a position in Moscow teaching English as a second language and would be gone for at least six months and maybe even for a year if it worked out. Wow! She continued to love Russian culture and was determined to be involved. She had always had a little rebellious streak in her and she wasn't going to let anyone like the FBI slow her down. I definitely wasn't going to bring that up again, or even tell her that I didn't think it was a good idea. It seemed as if Russia was turning on us again, and I feared for her safety in case a major conflict was to occur. I never talked about Arman or mentioned anything concerning my negative thoughts toward her Russian participation. I had come to be very cautious dealing with Russians, to put it mildly, although they were still at the top of Anna's list of favorite people.

Anna invited me to stay at her home while she was away because she was running a profitable Airbnb out of the upstairs, and our old dog Bruiser was with her. He had been with me for the past few years but had a flea problem that I couldn't get under control, so Anna agreed to take him. She promised that when she returned that she would seriously consider getting back together. I asked her if she was going to toss me out when she came back and told her that it would be hard for me to find a place especially when she didn't have a timeline. She assured me that she wouldn't throw me out without warning, and she would let me stay in the only spare room which was her art studio. As far as she was concerned, it was a humorous tongue in cheek conversation. (it seriously wasn't too funny for me).

I moved into Anna's house in early August 2017 and was to occupy the master bedroom when she left and manage the Airbnb, and she had a college student tenant at the time who was there for the entire summer. Bruiser was happy with me being there. It was an ideal situation, except for Anna not being there, with the house being on a nice quiet cove with a private shady backyard and porch. I had missed sitting outside drinking coffee in the mornings and hadn't been able to since my times in the Ozarks a couple of years earlier. The Airbnb tenant was hardly ever there and kept to herself, but the best thing about it was being on the Green Line, which was a walking and biking trail that went right through the heart of Memphis. I could ride one way fifteen minutes to arrive at one of the nicest parks around and fifteen minutes the other way to visit Natalie because her and Joe's house backed up to the Green Line.

CHAPTER 13

>¤<

Back in the USSR

*A*nna left for Moscow the day after I moved in, and her flight was delayed in Frankfort where she felt nauseated and then arrived in Moscow totally worn out and very queasy. Her month-long training was to begin the next day, and we were going to communicate through Skype and an app called Marco Polo. They were both free and she could have FaceTime with all of us at home. She had her iPhone cut off before she left, and I gave her the local phone that I used in Kazakhstan, and the minutes were very inexpensive. We didn't hear from Anna for the first couple days (typical adventurous Anna) and she finally messaged me on Skype and said that her stomach was still bothering her and her energy level was low, assuming it was jet lag.

Her training class was about ten hours each day with a very short break, and in the next message, she told me that she was zapped and was having a hard time walking from her flat to the class. Her nausea was worse, and she made me promise not to tell Natalie and Reid about her problem. We spoke with her FaceTime on Marco Polo about her fifth day and she appeared to be okay and her usual energetic self. The class continued through Saturday with Sundays being their only day off, but Sunday night was a homework night to prepare for the upcoming week. She attempted to go sightseeing Sunday but was too weak and confessed she still hadn't been able to keep anything on her stomach, assuming she might have picked up some type of virus.

She went to class Monday wondering if she could make it through the day. She said the class was demanding, and she was the youngest by about twenty-five years and was having doubts about passing the training. Anna had always been a winner and wasn't about to quit, and we assured her that it would be okay if she did, and she halfway considered it. The next day of her class she was supposed to conduct a practice teaching session, and she battled through the session and was almost too tired to stand up when she finished. Her roommate was very concerned and afraid she might be dehydrated and insisted she needed medical assistance.

Anna called her friend Marta who she had tried to aid in starting the Russian homecare business. They had become good friends, and Marta came and forced her to go straight to the emergency room. Anna was certainly dehydrated and they administered fluids, and after the first day she felt better but still couldn't keep anything on her stomach. They ran tests and couldn't figure out the root cause. Anna tried to fake being happy and feeling good on FaceTime, but she could barely walk, and it was noticeable that she was struggling. She was hoping to get her strength back and determined to get back to the training. In the hospital, Anna shared the room with several other ladies, and they had group meals, and she said she was treated well by the staff and especially her roommates who were supposed to watch out for each other. After quite a few tests, they treated her for stomach issues and released her, going back to her flat extremely weak.

Our friend Albert, who treated Reid, had been out of town and came to visit her the day she was released from the hospital. Anna couldn't eat solid food, and when she would try to walk she would have to throw up. Albert told her she needed to be back in the hospital and used his connections to get her into one of the finest hospitals in Moscow where she was immediately started back on fluids. Albert and his wife began communicating with us through email keeping us informed of the details and how the extensive tests couldn't come up with a diagnosis.

After another week in the hospital, Albert took her to his house by ambulance, and we decided we had to get her home and into our healthcare system in Memphis, which is the finest in the world (no brag, just fact). We looked at hiring a private medical jet, but even with a $50,000 discount it was going to cost $120,000, and it wasn't possible. We scheduled a first-class flight on a commercial jet with special attention and wheelchair escorts through the airports. Anna traveled by ambulance to the airport, still powerless to walk more than a few feet and so terribly sick. We prayed for her to get back to Memphis knowing it would be the most wearisome and painful trip of her life.

Anna arrived in Memphis about twenty hours later with no flight delays and Natalie, Joe, and I picked her up in their SUV. We rolled her to the car and helped her in, noticing her loss of weight and obvious fatigue. We wanted to take her straight to the emergency room, but she insisted she spent at least one night in her own bed. When we got to the house, Joe and I practically carried her to the sofa and that's as far as she could go and never made it to her bed. She was VERY, VERY sick!

We attempted to reach her primary care physician before she left Moscow, but he was out of town and not expected to be home until two days after Anna returned. The hospital in Russia had forwarded all of the test results to his office, and the next morning I called Anna's insurance company to find out the right emergency room because there was no way she could wait till the next day to see her doctor. When Anna woke up, I helped her change clothes and get into my car. Natalie had to be back to work after staying up all night. When we pulled up to the emergency room entrance, I quickly rolled her in with a wheelchair, and after a blood test, they put her on fluids. The young doctor came back and diagnosed her with a thyroid problem and believed it to be causing all of her problems. She was already taking thyroid medication and he thought an adjustment would be the solution and kept her there on fluids for a few hours and released her.

We were scratching our heads wondering how this could be the problem, and before we got back to the house, Anna's doctor's nurse called and said that she had received the records and reached her doctor on vacation. He believed that the test showed that Anna's

Hepatitis C had returned and ordered us to go straight to the hospital. The nurse called ahead, and we made a U-turn and headed straight to another hospital which we were very familiar with and would for sure take Anna's insurance. It was right after lunch when they assigned her a room and immediately started fluids and drew blood. In a few hours, the hospitalist came back and said that it wasn't hepatitis, but her breast cancer had come back and metastasized to her bones. I knew we had to tell Natalie but realized she would be shaken to the core, so I called Joe and told him he needed to come with her when she got off work. Reid would take it hard also, but Natalie was very emotional and always felt things strongly and very deeply. Reid is so much like me, not very emotional and tends to hold things in.

There was one major problem because her symptoms weren't the usual signs of cancer coming back, and they ran more tests and MRIs and came up with nothing to explain the nausea. Natalie came to the hospital and was brave and composed, and we all prayed for Anna's healing and wisdom for the doctors. I went home and got Anna's pajamas and personal items and called Reid, knowing that they were going to keep her. I brought my overnight bag because there was no way for her to be left alone, and we weren't going to leave her side. As sick as she was, she always waited for me to assist her with the vomit bag and never made a mess.

Over the next couple of days, Anna developed excruciating headaches and began to see double, and every time she moved or tried to sit up she would get nauseated and need to throw up. She had a wonderful team of specialists trying to figure out what was causing the headaches, but it was still a horrible mystery. The number 1 goal was to get her strong enough to start chemo for the already late stage four cancer. I had noticed before she left for Moscow when we would come back from our bike rides that she would need to rest for a minute which was quite unusual for her. She would always get ahead with me having to catch up and could ride for miles, so we thought nothing of her being a little tired.

I was still selling golf clubs and told my boss that I needed a few days off, and that was no problem. I thank God that I took early social security and could afford to miss. Natalie and Joe were working high-pressure jobs and had already used most of their vacation days, but Natalie would come faithfully after work, with Joe running errands for us. She would relieve me while I went home and checked on our Airbnb guest, Bruiser, and showered, and then I'd go back and spend the night and next day with Anna.

After all of our time in the homecare business, I had never seen anyone suffer like Anna, and I didn't see how she could continue. Morphine was the only drug that could take the edge off of her headache pain, and she was getting it intravenously every four hours. Anna's dad, who was eighty-three years old, came and spent the day on Friday while I went home and crashed. Natalie relieved him and stayed Friday night after work. I couldn't stay away, so I came back for a while to see Natalie and catch up with what the doctors were saying. Reid was working and living in Pennsylvania and was checking with us daily. He wanted to be there, but it was impossible, and I reminded him that I would always let him know if it was time to come home.

By Sunday, Anna was hydrated and able to keep a little food down, and the goal was for her to visit the cancer center and begin chemo. Before they released her, they performed a spinal tap and an MRI on her brain to check for cancer that might be causing the headaches, and thankfully the tests all came back negative. She was elated to get out of the hospital, and they sent her home with extremely strong pain medicine and nausea suppositories that basically knocked her out.

As soon as we were back home, Anna wasn't able to hold any food down, and Anna's dad returned to Memphis from his home in Selmer to assist. He was battling with cancer himself, multiple myeloma, and was undergoing chemo which was keeping it at bay. He was torn to pieces seeing Anna like this having been through it with her mom just a year earlier. Natalie and he were able to get Anna in the shower, sitting on a metal chair, which made her feel better. Homehealth sent a wheelchair home with us, but she was too weak to transfer herself or get dressed. She had an appointment at the cancer center with the doctor who had treated her previous cancer,

Dr. Schwartzberg, and we felt like he was the very best. We were very impressed with him and one of his staff had been in to see her every day in the hospital.

During our time in the hospital, we were overwhelmed with support from friends who brought food to the house, allowing us to not worry about meals. At least two hundred from all over the country and friends from overseas were praying daily for her on Facebook.

We were scheduled to see Dr. Schwartzberg on Wednesday, and fortunately he was coming back in town Monday night. Tuesday we had an appointment to come in for tests and blood work to determine the proper plan of care and the best chemo formula. Tuesday morning Anna's dad and I got her in the backseat of his car, but she couldn't sit and had to lie down. We hurried to get to the center because Anna was experiencing the unexplainable nausea. We took her up to the lab on the second floor in a wheelchair holding the vomit bag, and she was unable to get in the seat in the lab.

As it turned out Dr. Schwartzberg's physician's assistant, Liz had gone to church with us and remembered Anna well. She still kept a devotional that Anna had given her on her nightstand. Liz called upstairs to the infusion room to see if there was a bed available in that constantly busy place. Liz found one and immediately started the fluids with anti-nausea, steroids, and strong pain medicine enabling us to take Anna home very weak but more comfortable.

Her double vision and headaches had progressively gotten worse, and she had about fifteen pills at home for various needs. Natalie kept them very organized, and I gave different ones to her three times a day along with strong pain medicine every four hours. Anna wasn't able to read the labels clearly enough to take the right ones, and I remained by her side 24-7 at home and became her primary caregiver. Natalie was there more than she needed to be, getting worn out, and being very concerned for her mom, became a cancer research expert. Reid was texting daily and I was trying to be as positive with him as possible while still being truthful. He was wanting to get home but also had no vacation left. We were all so worried, but Anna kept fighting and amazed us by her never complaining attitude and was more concerned for the kids than for herself.

The next day Anna's dad was worn out, needing a break, and headed back to Selmer. I loaded her in the back seat and got her to the lab on the second floor at the cancer center, and Natalie took off work for a few hours and met us there. Again, Liz wheeled her to a bed in the infusion area since she still wasn't able to sit up. Our goal of starting chemo that morning wasn't going to be met. Dr. Schwartzberg came in, and again they immediately gave her IV pain meds, fluids, and steroids. He sent us back to the hospital to be on powerful steroids to hopefully get Anna strong enough to tolerate chemo. He also placed orders for an ophthalmologist to examine her eyes and for a neurologist to do a brain scan to determine what was causing the nausea, headaches, and double vision. This was a puzzle for the finest doctors in Memphis. All we knew to do was pray, and Anna always welcomed it.

I drove Anna directly back to Baptist East Hospital with her lying down in the back seat. They immediately whisked her in for a brain scan and for another MRI. The ophthalmologist came and gave her an eye exam which was very painful when he directed her to look from one side to the other or up and down. The MRI results came back late that afternoon with some more tough news revealing that the cancer had spread to a tiny muscle in her eye. Even though it wasn't the news we were praying for, they had found the cause of the symptoms. The ophthalmologist returned the next morning with an eye patch to alternate covering each eye, which was a major break-through. By the next day, the double vision cleared up as long as she was wearing the patch.

The neurologist stopped by to see her that day and created a non-narcotic cocktail mix for her headaches. They persisted, but were tolerable, and she was able to get off the morphine, which she had been taking every four hours around the clock. Anna and all of us were so happy with this positive step forward. She was still too weak to walk, but after two more days of steroids, and being able to eat solid food for the first time in almost two months, she was able to take short strolls. She could make it to the bathroom and back and go forty or fifty feet without sitting down in her wheelchair which we always had right behind her. She was hurting in places that seemed to move around on her body, so they prescribed a permanent fentanyl patch.

What helped her relax was me giving her good old-fashioned back scratches and rubs which she looked forward to. She seemed to truly miss me when I wasn't with her and was beginning to depend on me (it was probably the back scratches which she had loved for thirty years). She always wanted to know when I was coming back, and we were able to speak very frankly with each other about what she was going through. Her main concern was whether she would ever be able to do art, drive, or ride her bike again, and I assured her that I knew in my heart that she would. She began to believe it and never gave in one inch in the battle.

Natalie and I had to help each other keep up with the daily changing details concerning her cancer. They decided to give Anna her first chemo treatment as soon as she was healthy enough. They wanted to keep her and begin the treatment where they could observe her, avoiding another trip back if she didn't react well. She had been there seven days this time, and they came Monday to put in a porta cathe, and Anna insisted that I stay in the room with her.

I kind of jokingly said, "I might see your titties?"

She seriously answered, "You have seen them before, and I need you to stay. I'm so afraid!"

I told her that I loved her a few times, and she would respond that she loved me in some kind of way. I would always tell her that I would be there as long as she needed me, and she would say that she did and sincerely wanted me to be with her. Really, neither one of us had much choice unless Natalie or Reid risked losing their jobs, and I wasn't going to leave her unless she called security to haul me off.

The golf shop told me that my job would be there waiting on me when, or if, I came back. It was no coincidence how God miraculously, through these horrible circumstances, put us back together, and no one can ever convince me otherwise. God is very real! I had been praying for Him to use me again, somehow, and bring me back into some type of ministry, but this wasn't quite what I had pictured.

Although Anna never complained, she would tell me that she was scared and had thoughts of being in this condition forever. I did the best I could to encourage her, and we both believed she would whip the cancer as did Natalie and Reid and our praying friends. Anna's dad wasn't as hopeful and had been in touch with his brother who was a radiologist. He had studied the test results and believed she had less than a year to live, but I certainly didn't tell Anna, Natalie or Reid that. The average lifespan for metastatic breast cancer was two to three years but Anna was certainly in no way average. Some of Dr. Schwartzberg's patients had lived over ten years with the disease and there were new treatments coming out almost daily, and not beating the cancer was never an option for Anna or us. They proceeded with the first chemo treatment with no negative reactions and released Anna the next day. We were all happy to have her back home, and she was due for the next chemo treatment in a week.

CHAPTER 14

※

Light Coming out of the Darkness

*A*nna was resting after breakfast the next morning, and I was sitting down just pondering (I'm a pro at that). I felt strongly that I was to pray for Anna, and I wasn't sure how to pray, but about fifteen or so years ago God had given us a prayer language. It is a spiritual gift, and sometimes I would pray that way to thank God or pray when I just didn't have the words myself. Anna occasionally was able to interpret the language. I went into the bedroom and asked her, "Can I pray for you in tongues?" She agreed and I just poured out my heart to the Lord, and after a few minutes, Anna broke down and began to sob. Anna literally hardly ever cried, not even about her cancer or anything that I could remember.

She pulled herself together and said, "There is something I have to tell you, Mike. The reason that I pulled away from you was because of Arman! We fell in love and have been involved with each other as long as you and I have been apart. Since dad and my brothers forced me to cut him off, it isn't even possible for us to be friends. I promise it's over." He was still married and living with his wife, who we had previously helped leave Uzbekistan. She sobbed again and asked me, "Is there any way that you can forgive me? I really want for us to be together again."

I said, "YES" and chill bumps went all over me. That was the beginning of her loving me emotionally again and would take time. It was God's Amazing Grace. I asked her, "Will you forgive me for not being the husband I should have been and not showing you daily that I loved and appreciated you?"

She said, "YES!" We agreed that the past was in the past and that it was a brand new day for us. I have struggled to forgive Arman. I still question his motives and feel betrayed by him in the worst way imaginable. Through much prayer and thinking about the consequences of somehow getting even, I have finally been able to forgive him in my heart (although I still wouldn't be too bothered if the fleas of a thousand camels infested his armpits). I do feel a release from the bitterness which can lead to a dark and destructive path. I can remember my dad saying on several occasions when he was my age if confronted with similar urges, "I'm too old to fight. I'd have to hurt 'im," and now I know exactly what he was talking about. I am trying to empathize with Arman's situation and realize that he came from a communist society where many don't view marriage the way we do. In my opinion, he was playing a dangerous role scripted by his superiors.

Our friends continued to bring meals and constantly offered assistance. Several of Anna's friends visited her in the hospital when she was able, and my best friend from high school prayed daily for us and sent me encouraging daily texts.

The third day after returning from the hospital, Anna had an appointment with a specialist at The UT Research Center. His objective was to review the eye tests and determine if the tumor on her eye muscle would respond to radiation and if it could be done safely. Anna was able to transfer in and out of the car by herself, but we had to stop on the way because she was getting dizzy. She had spent too much time with the patch off earlier, and she had to lay down on the backseat. When we arrived to check in, Anna felt like she was going to pass out. They were able to get her to a bed while waiting for the doctor. An elderly doctor walked in who turned out to be the director of the entire center and was a close friend of Dr. Schwartzberg. He was so kind and gentle as he examined her eyes, as it was painful for her to move them. He smiled at Anna and told her that he believed that radiation would shrink the tumor, and she wouldn't see double anymore. The only negative was that she would have to do the chemo for eight more weeks to get the tumor smaller. We thought this was glorious news, and Anna began to be thrilled about the prospect of seeing and living once again.

Anna was too weary to walk that afternoon but forced herself to make it to the kitchen and back. She wanted to sit on the sofa and try to draw. Her favorite art mode of the day was drawing and painting mandalas and Zentangles (really cool, you should Google it). She would sit with the patch on one eye and began to draw intricate patterns. Natalie and I were fascinated by her drive and zeal for even attempting to do this. She was elated and felt blessed, but after a while she would get dizzy and have to stop. The new headache medicine was working and was basically a cocktail of caffeine and several non-narcotics that doctors were prescribing for migraines. At bedtime she would start with that, but after a few hours she would need something stronger to get through the night.

Thursday when it was time for chemo, Anna still wasn't able to walk all the way to the car. It seemed like the first treatment didn't have many side effects except the nagging fatigue. Anna was sick when we arrived and, once again, needed to lie down in the infusion room. The treatment went well and we didn't have to come back the next Thursday. This treatment was set up to be two weeks on and one week off, as long as it was working, from then on (yep, forever).

Through Natalie's ongoing research, she was finding out from friends and their family members who had suffered from cancer that medical marijuana alleviated symptoms and even killed some of the cells. Anna was willing to try it, and I wasn't planning on stopping her. The CBD oil was legally available and doesn't have the THC that gets you high, so we ordered a bottle and began to give Anna one drop per day. I asked one of the other cancer center doctors what he thought, and he said that it wouldn't hurt, but he couldn't prescribe it until it was approved by the FDA. Most of the people who had success with the marijuana had actually used the normal kind with THC, along with the drops. Most used the edible forms that were for specific types of cancer. We were realizing how bad Anna felt and how the narcotics were knocking her out and bad for her liver, so Natalie wanted Anna to try it.

She was offered some of the edibles that were left over from a friend's mother's treatment, who had combined it with the chemo, and it truly helped the nausea and pain symptoms. Then Natalie said something that caused my eyes to bug out! She wanted me to be the guinea pig before giving it to her mom. Natalie didn't indulge and knew that I had in the past, and I told her that I would volunteer (right or wrong?). I was willing if it could give Anna some relief, and I sampled it right before I left to get some prescriptions filled. By the time I got to the drug store, I was relaxed and had a very interesting experience waiting on the refills and driving home listening to the radio. Anna would partake from time to time, and it truly made her feel better, especially when she was in a lot of pain and had zero energy. I can't do it because I enjoy it too much, and it would be an all-day, everyday thing for me, and I don't feel right doing it. God emphatically told me it was wrong for me that time in high school when I missed the field goal, so until I hear different, I don't feel right partaking.

Anna was getting her strength back, and we would find out the next Thursday if the chemo was having a positive effect. Over the weekend, she wanted to go to Ikea to get a new living room chair, hoping to make her living area as pleasant as possible, since she would be spending many days there in the foreseeable future. She wasn't the type to sit around for any period over a few minutes and was always involved in some type of project, often more than one. She never watched a lot of TV and was annoyed when the kids and I lay around watching the tube, thinking we were wasting valuable time. We went to Ikea on Saturday and bought a cool chair (only took me about six hours to put it together). While at the store Anna developed a severe pain in her chest which subsided in about five minutes. We were alarmed and called her nurse, and she said that it was either the cancer or the chemo, probably the chemo. This happened again quite a few times. While I put the chair together, she worked on her art and was amused with my frustration until her head started hurting.

Anna was getting strength back over the next few days and was able to walk almost a block. She was able to get in the shower by herself and able to cook a little, with my assistance. Although we still didn't have to worry about meals, Natalie came up with nutritious recipes and insisted that we eat healthy to the utmost extreme. The angriest Natalie ever was with me was when she discovered that I had cooked Anna some frozen French fries. What a mean look she gave me, unlike any I had seen before. This infraction of mine prompted her and Joe to stop by earlier every night and help me with the new healthy menu. I was making Anna and myself fruit smoothies with yogurt and other additives, which I had no clue what they were, for breakfast.

There were three or four faithful friends that would come spend time with Anna while I went to the store to get items on Natalie's list, or just went somewhere and chilled for a bit. She still couldn't stay by herself because she had fallen several times and was unable to stand up without help. She would get out of breath and dizzy and the shortness of breath was becoming more and more a hindrance to the pace she was determined to keep.

We went to the lab before chemo Thursday, as we did before each treatment, and received wonderful results. The cancer markers were down substantially, and this was such comforting news for all of us, and I was so thrilled to text Reid and tell him. Anna had been able to walk all the way from the parking lot into the clinic, and for the first time was able to sit in the regular chair. The treatments didn't take but about forty-five minutes, but the wait was sometimes long, and Anna would bring her iPad for backgammon games. The trip to the center and back would usually take three or four hours, and Anna would be exhausted and need to lie down when we got back to the house. We had a week off before going back again. It was a welcome break and helped all of us take our minds off of the West Clinic, wonderful as it was, it could be quite depressing seeing all the desperate, hurting patients.

There was more fantastic news when Reid called, and he was going to come to Memphis the next weekend, and this was the most excited we had seen Anna. The chemo symptoms would usually hit Anna the following Monday after the Thursday treatments so Anna was hoping she would have plenty of energy for the visit. Reid's girl-friend, Madison, who we adore, was going to be able to come also.

Reid arrived Friday night and Anna was pumped, but she fell down the next day from standing up and walking too quickly. She needed to get her bearings before walking and often took off before she remembered to do this. She was okay, and Joe and Reid helped her up and got her to bed. Even with the eye patch it was hard for her to focus, and Reid was discovering firsthand what a difficult time she was having. One of the greatest moments of my life occured the next day when we took a picture of us all together as a family once again. I had a very rare emotional moment and was flooded with joy and tears, and it remains my favorite photo of all time!

A physical therapist was coming by two times a week and stopped by Sunday and went through the therapy with Reid cheering Anna on. While going through the routine, the horrible chest pain came back violently and didn't go away. Anna's blood pressure spiked past the danger zone and the PT told us to call 911, which I did and we cleared the way. The EMTs arrived quickly and rushed Anna to the hospital with us following in two cars. Shortly after being seen at the ER, the pain subsided and her blood pressure suddenly normalized. After a CT scan and blood work revealed no heart attack or stroke, they released her. What happened was another mystery, and they suggested she see a cardiologist ASAP to try to find a diagnosis. I stood in the driveway the next morning and watched Reid head out, worried about his mom, knowing how difficult this was for him.

We went to a cardiologist and after a full examination, she said Anna's heart was as healthy as anybody's she had seen and had no answers. The chest pains were still a mystery and she would continue to have them periodically but never that severe, and at least we had a sense that the chest pains weren't life threatening. Anna was beginning to create more artwork and was turning out some beautiful pieces, and we were all wondering what she would accomplish with two eyes (so was she).

The next visit to the cancer center proved the chemo was working, as the markers were down again, but there was negative news. Her liver numbers were up substantially. They had been slightly high, but not enough for concern. They scheduled an ultrasound and completed it before we left, and Dr. Schwartzberg didn't notice anything abnormal. He scheduled an appointment with a gastro doctor who was a leading liver expert for a second opinion. He saw something slightly unusual but said that if it was cancer, the chemo she was receiving would be what he would prescribe. Dr. Schwartzberg looked at the results again and said he still didn't see anything but would keep a close watch on it.

Anna and I were enjoying each other's company more and more and were laughing and having fun together and played backgammon almost every morning. Anna's only option was winning, and she trashed talked better than any NBA athlete I had ever heard. This was constant through every game we played and on the few occasions when I would win, she would sulk and pout for the next hour. It was almost worth letting her win, but my competitive spirit wouldn't allow it and, like my dad, I had never even played tiddlywinks for fun. We also decided that we would go out and do one fun thing every day such as going to an art supply store or coffee shop. She actually persuaded me to begin drawing Zentangles and even though mine looked like kindergarten productions, it was something we could do together, and I really enjoyed it. I still do.

Going to Shelby Farms and walking was one of our favorite activities, and Anna was beginning to be able to outdistance me. My groin pain was worse and my knees hurt bad, and often I would sit on a bench, and she would make it all the way around a large lake. It was getting harder for me to get in and out of the car and put on my shoes and socks. It was strange because Anna could make longer treks some days and others she would be weak and short of breath. We assumed it was from the chemo because it occurred more often the fourth and next few days after treatment.

It was time for a full body scan, and the results showed that the cancer wasn't spreading except for spots that appeared in her abdomen. It would be another month before they would check the tumor in her eye to see if it was ready for radiation, and she was getting frustrated wanting to be able to drive and to draw with both eyes. She hated having to have someone with her, having everyone think she needed a babysitter, but she allowed us to do it without resisting.

Every time I thought I might be able to go back to work, at least part time, something would come up that would make it impossible for her to be alone for more than a few hours. There was no way to have any regular work schedule. I was still doing finances for the lady who had lost her husband because I could do it at home on my own schedule. This work was slowing down though because she was past ready to retire and was beginning to phase it out. I was so glad that I took social security at age sixty-two, and it turned out to be the perfect timing. Anna was my top priority, and I knew things would work out financially.

Anna would tell me every once and a while that she was becoming more and more fond of me, and I understood that it wasn't easy for her to get over her feelings for Arman. We were loving each other by faith, and the emotions were starting to come back, and I was actually starting to feel a heartfelt romantic love for her again. Only God can stir up that type of love between two people that had been through what we had, and we both believed that we were supposed to be together and were trusting God to see it through.

CHAPTER 15

—◆※◆—

Fighting the Monster

*A*nna appeared to be improving and had gone almost a week without dizziness or shortness of breath. We went back to Ikea, and she was able to walk through the store without the wheelchair. This time she wanted a large dining room table that could also serve as an art station, and we found the perfect one on sale. It took me seven hours this time to assemble it with Anna hoping I would get frustrated and cuss. It went fairly smooth since I had gotten used to the Ikea assembly system, but there was a problem. Anna's favorite cat ever had passed away right before she left for Moscow, and she really wanted another one, and Natalie agreed that we should start looking. I am not an indoor cat person, but I surrendered, and we found a rescue that was incredibly sweet (in the beginning). This little rascal immediately started intimidating Bruiser and making him get out of his bed. Like myself, Bruiser was too old to fight and allowed Misty to take complete advantage of him. This kitten would sneak up and steal nuts and bolts while assembling the table, if I looked away for two seconds. I let an off color one slip (little bastard) and Anna's wish came true.

Christmas was right around the corner and Reid was coming home! He worked for a logistics company which operated 24-7, so his days off would be about a week before Christmas. This visit was more encouraging for Reid, and he definitely witnessed improvement in Anna. They were able to get out and about and spend some quality time together, with Anna actually feeling more like her normal self. It was her off week from treatment with no scary events happening like on his previous visit. She was starting to take it a little easier and was beginning to accept the fact that she couldn't always go full speed.

We had a tremendous family Christmas celebration together allowing Reid to head back to Pennsylvania much more relaxed and confident that Anna was going to improve. Natalie and I thought Anna was turning the corner, and the plan of care was working. Shortly after Reid left, we went to the cancer center and found out terrific news that radiation on the eye muscle could begin the first week of January.

Christmas Sunday was approaching and Anna was ready to find a church home, feeling like she could sit through an hour and a half service. Natalie and Joe had been visiting different churches and suggested we go to High Point Church. The service was wonderful, and it was the best Christmas message that I have heard preached (have heard a bunch of them). Anna was truly touched and wanted to go down for prayer during the invitation, and I am sure it was a good prayer, but the music was so loud that we couldn't hear a word that was said. On the way out the minister that prayed for her was standing at the door and come to find out, his wife was Dr. Schwartzberg's head nurse. She was able to give Anna a little extra attention and encouragement at the cancer center in the coming months along with, Liz, his PA. It was God's loving touch and not a coincidence, and Anna knew He had His eye on her.

When the actual Christmas Day rolled around, Anna, Natale, Joe and I went to Selmer and spent the entire holiday weekend together with my in-laws. It was so precious for all of us to be there for a few days as a family, just like before the divorce. Anna enjoyed herself but was starting to get tired easier and didn't have the energy that she had the past two weeks.

Anna's brother, Ben, who lived in Oakland, CA, gave us a trip for Christmas to Hot Springs, AR to enjoy the bathhouses and massages. He had flown into Memphis several times during the past months and had been a blessing and available for whatever we needed him to do. We had wanted to get away for a short vacation, and now we believed that Anna would feel like it and planned the trip before she started the radiation. We had been there quite a few times for short getaways in the past, and it was a very quaint little town in the mountains with a lot of history and plenty to do, so we were looking very much forward to it.

Anna had another chemo treatment on Thursday and we were going to head to Hot Springs on the following Monday morning. Her symptoms weren't as bad after the last round, but as soon as we pulled out of the driveway, Anna experienced another chest pain attack. It didn't last long, but she got dizzy and needed to lay down on the back seat, feeling discouraged. By the time we arrived, she wasn't ready to get up and enjoy the day, and since I am being honest here, I had brought along a "special" medical rice crispy treat. She hadn't had one like this before, so I decided I would take a bite and after about twenty minutes it didn't seem to have any bad effects. I gave her a substantially bigger bite and helped her out of the car. We walked a short distance to a very cool little sandwich shop and ordered the healthiest sandwich on the menu along with some sweet potato fries. About the time the food came, Anna chuckled and said, "Hey, I feel better! That treat was very, very nice." We started getting tickled and could barely stop laughing. We finished eating and walked around a for a minute and had some true belly laughs. I sat on a bench while Anna went in the rock and souvenir shops and she was having a blast. After she finished shopping and bought something for everybody at home, we headed for our Airbnb. The next day Anna felt much better, and we enjoyed the baths and hour long massages, and it was a relaxing, much needed getaway. Now it was time to get back to reality and resume the battle against the relentless monster called cancer.

Anna began the radiation treatments, and if they were successful, she would accomplish what she feared she would never take on again. She would be able to ride her bike, drive, and paint with both eyes, and most importantly, regain some independence. She had been faithfully wearing the patch on one eye and had produced as much art work as she had in the previous two years, but if she spent too much time drawing or watching TV, her headaches would return.

She hadn't had a strong pain pill in several weeks and the non-narcotic medicine continued to work. She was still taking twelve pills a day for other symptoms, which Natalie helped me keep organized and filled.

If the radiation was successful her double vision would clear up in two to three weeks, and we were all praying. The radiation didn't seem to bother her, and two weeks after the treatments were completed her vision started to improve, and she was able to go without the patch for short periods of time. By the end of the third week she could see normally again! The first thing she wanted to do was go on a short bike ride, and she grabbed her backpack and put some hedge clippers in it. Before she went to Moscow, she had noticed some bamboo along the Green Line, and after riding about a quarter mile she spotted it. She climbed off her bike and cut some, and then we went riding off with bamboo rising out of her backpack. This was Anna being totally herself unhindered by the cancer, and it was a tremendous breakthrough. She went on short drives in the car but hit a curb one time and realized she had to be extremely careful (so did we). She had beaten the cancer back and was going full speed ahead with the zip back in her step.

My groin pain was getting worse, and I went for my yearly physical and told my doctor that the bladder and hernia surgeries didn't help, and she decided to do a hip X-ray. The results showed my right hip joint was totally worn out, bone on bone, and I was relieved to know the cause of the pain. Apparently I was about two years overdue for a hip replacement, and it was good timing for me to have the procedure because Anna was stable and could take care of her personal needs. I had out outpatient surgery and the recovery, thankfully, was fast with the pain totally gone. I started PT and Anna's dad came and stayed with us for a few days running errands and taking me to therapy. I was able to hit golf balls in three weeks and felt like a bionic man and don't know why I didn't realize it was my hip all the time.

Anna's cancer markers had stabilized but weren't getting lower and it was early February 2018. Anna was asked if she wanted to assist with her former art instructor job and happily accepted the challenge and allowed me to take her and pick her up. It was exhausting, but she was so encouraged and even went back the next week and instructed a class herself.

She hadn't needed the headache medicine since regaining her full site, but a setback was right around the corner. Anna woke up with excruciating back pain and was unable to stand or get dressed by herself, so I called Liz and got her into the wheelchair and to the center. This was the first time she had to use the chair in two months and was thinking she had told it goodbye. I thought she had ruptured a disk because excruciating pain was going down her legs, and she could barely stand up. A CT scan showed nothing abnormal, and they scheduled an appointment with a physical therapist and prescribed muscle relaxers to add to her long list of meds. They didn't seem to help, and she had to take the stronger pain pills again for the first time in a month after thinking she had also said goodbye to them. They increased the dosage on her fentanyl patch which she had worn from day one. The next day when we went to PT, Anna wasn't able to walk in, and they massaged her lower back and made adjustments. Anna showed improvement that night, and we went back two more times, and the pain vanished as fast as it came. Whew!

We always prayed for healing and for her to have good days better than the one before, and she was still enjoying beating me at backgammon every morning and was starting to create some intricate Zentangles. She was using the bamboo to make cigar box art and her artistic ability was blossoming. Several of her lady friends stopped by occasionally, and she would teach them some of her favorite techniques. I was able to get back out on the golf course a few times and was thinking I could soon get back to part time work.

It was time for another full body scan, and some spots appeared under one of her breasts and more in her abdomen. The cancer had been extensive throughout her skeletal system since first being diagnosed in September. We had noticed her abdomen was starting to swell noticeably, and her liver numbers were up substantially again. There were four or five small spots on her liver, but the current chemo was the best treatment, and it was keeping the cancer at bay.

Anna was starting to feel weak and out of breath again and found herself struggling to get up and be active. She was doing the physical therapy exercises every morning and getting to her art table, and we were determined to continue to get her out of the house and do at least one fun thing every day, such as going on short bike rides. Natalie and Joe continued to stop by just about every night and kept her entertained and humored, and I was finally learning to cook something besides microwave popcorn and was able to make simple healthy lunches and dinners. Every once and a while we would sneak away and get something unhealthy, but Natalie would somehow find out. She was bringing kombucha and other drinks I had never heard of and would sit and watch Anna drink them. Anna really started to crave ice cream and I would try to hide goodies in the back of the freezer. Most food tasted weird to her since beginning the chemo, but she loved the deserts and an occasional greasy hamburger.

Changing the chemo to a different formula was being considered now, and they sent us back to the liver specialist to determine if something besides the cancer was elevating the liver enzymes. He performed a biopsy and it was definitely cancer affecting the liver, and he continued to believe that chemo was the best treatment available. She was beginning to get frustrated and angry because of her lack of energy, and we all encouraged her and told her this was just another bump in the road, which she was going to conquer.

Spring of 2018 was right around the corner and we went to get some outdoor plants and flowers, which Anna loved and always enjoyed tending to. Each day she made sure she got a few planted, and I watched her scurry around in amazement thinking, "How is it even possible for her to do that?"

The next blood work revealed that the chemo wasn't working, the cancer markers being up for the first time since she started treatment. It would be a week before the doctor could start her on a different type, and he was also looking for new experimental drugs that seemed to be coming out almost weekly. This was discouraging and we were all fearful because time was not on our side.

The following week, the day before we received the news about another form of treatment, I received a FB message from a longtime family friend. She said that the Indian pastor, Joel, who Anna had ministered with in India was in town. He wanted to come see us while in Memphis, and I picked him up early the next morning and brought him to our home. Anna was very happy to see him and he told Anna, "I have been trying to reach you for several years."

Anna responded, "I have been running from God and was embarrassed to talk to you."

Joel, with a big broad grin on his face, blurted out, "Run back to Him right now!"

Anna happily replied, "Okay, I will!"

He was aware of our divorce and asked, "Are you back together?"

Anna said, "We are reconciling."

He asked, "Do you want to get married again now?"

We told him enthusiastically, "We sure would!"

We recited our vows and when Joel asked if Anna if she would take me till death do us part, she said, "Yes!" I looked at her with a surprised look and she said, "I mean it with all of my heart."

He pronounced us man and wife and started jumping up and down for joy! What a moment. God had answered my prayers and did what we thought was impossible and everyone was thrilled with this exciting news, beyond measure because our family was truly back together again. WOW!

We went to the cancer center with a new sense of hope and peace, knowing that God was in control, and they started Anna on a different chemo formula that would hopefully attack the cancer. Anna proved again to be double negative and couldn't be treated with the successful hormone therapies. It would be two more weeks before we knew if the new chemo would work, which she tolerated, but the side effects seem to sap her energy. Anna had lost most, but not all, of her hair and decided not to shave it, like when she had the breast cancer years ago. She found several pretty scarves and always tied them creatively. She had lost all of her eyelashes and the hair on her eyebrows, but maybe the new drug wouldn't affect her that way, and the hair would grow back.

Anna was still trucking along, and several friends came and picked her up one evening and went and made pottery. One lady had never done it before, and Anna helped her make something really cool that she was proud of. The ladies continued stopping by to do art with her, and one is still drawing Zentangles discovering a latent talent she didn't know she had. Two of the ladies were introduced through ministering to Anna, and they became good friends and continue to hang out.

The logistics company Reid was working for in Pennsylvania was going through some big changes, and he saw the writing on the wall and decided it was time to make a move. He had fallen in love with Colorado while on vacation there the past summer, and an opening became available with a company in Boulder that seemed like a good fit. He was also interviewing with a company in Atlanta that would be a brighter career move and better paying, but would also be more stressful working in an area of logistics that he wasn't familiar with. He didn't really want to live in Atlanta, but something super positive about it would be its much closer proximity to Memphis. He would also be on a regular Monday to Friday work schedule, and we could visit any weekend we wanted, and he chose Atlanta and began to search for housing. We were pleased he would be so much closer to home, and Anna was so happy it worked out that way, even though she was praying for the best move for him and his career.

She began making plans for a summer family vacation in Colorado and found a cool cabin on the edge of the Rocky Mountain National Park. It would be a reunion of us all together again, and our hope and prayer was that she would have enough energy to make the trip and enjoy herself. We reserved the cabin and bought the plane tickets, and Anna researched hiking trails and activities in the area.

Anna was pushing through the weariness and continued to create new pieces of art. We thought it was phenomenal what she had done with one eye, and now her art was even more expressive with tiny details. Her abdomen was noticeably expanding and becoming more and more uncomfortable, and she was beginning to have sharp pain under her rib cage. The "special" edibles seemed to help the most and increased her energy level, and she would only need a strong pain pill when she would wake up hurting during the night.

CHAPTER 16

⋙✦⋘

Will the Circle Be Unbroken

Besides praying, I felt like my main job was to keep her encouraged and to be positive for her and our family. It is so easy to get down, but Anna stayed up for the most part, and I have never seen anybody fight like she did. She was an encouragement and testimony to others with a smile on her face along with her own peculiar style of dry wit and humor. Our family and friends know exactly what I mean. She especially enjoyed making pokes at me, and we were usually able to make some kind of fun out of the circumstances.

Anna was bound and determined to ride her bike. We had convinced her that it wasn't safe for her to drive until she felt better again, and she reluctantly agreed. We got the bikes out of the garage, and I convinced her to take a test ride to the end of our cove. When she came back to the house, she stopped the bike and waited for me, she wasn't able to hold the bike up and fell off scraping her arm and knee. Thankfully she was wearing her helmet. She was okay, and we went inside and cleaned and bandaged the scrapes, and she was unfazed and remarkably not discouraged!

We went back to the center with Anna looking like she had been in a tussle. The staff was happy she was getting out and gave us the results about the new chemo. The cancer and liver markers were up and they were disturbed about the swelling in her abdomen and sent her downstairs for a CT scan. The scan showed more pronounced places on her liver, and the cancer had spread to her spleen.

Dr. Schwartzberg, always calm and positive, adjusted the chemo with hopes for the best.

I called Reid and told him, and he was in the process of moving to Atlanta and was to start his new job the next week. I assured him that even with this news that he needed to go to work and not come home, YET. Anna talked to him and ask him to not jeopardize his new career. They had given him extra time to start the job, allowing him to hear back from the Colorado offer, and it was time for him to prove himself. Natalie was shaken but was able to be positive with Anna, many times walking out of the living room and breaking down for a few minutes with Joe holding her. There has never been a daughter care for her mother the way Natalie did for Anna, as far as I have ever witnessed, and I knew Reid would have been with her daily if he hadn't lived many miles away.

Anna was usually mentally as sharp as a tack, and I noticed her beginning to be a little confused. On Friday she started thinking it was lunch time instead of dinner, and by Saturday night she wasn't eating and too weak to get out of the bed. Sunday afternoon she was calling me Wallace, her older brother's name, when we would try to sit her up in the bed, and it was very painful for her to move. We phoned the doctor on call and he told us to go to the emergency room for fluids and tests to figure out what was happening. She was also having the intense chest and abdominal pains, and the emergency room doctor told us her liver numbers were off the chart and said there was nothing left to do. Anna appeared to be resting and asleep, and I walked out in the hall and told Dr. No Tact not to talk like that in front of her because she was certainly listening. He said he believed in being totally honest, and I just shook my head.

I went with Anna to get the CT scan and she looked up at me with a grin on her face and said, "What that doctor said sounds pretty dire."

I told her, "He doesn't know for sure because he isn't a cancer specialist. Hopefully after the test they will be able to treat you for what is happening now." We called and got Reid on the phone and let him talk to her, and she called him Wallace and then laughed and quickly corrected herself. She spoke with him very sensibly and seemed to be coming back around a little bit. We convinced Reid to start work the next morning, and he would be able to come Friday, as planned, or as soon as we told him it was time to head home.

Anna's vitals were normal, and they checked her into a room, and the next morning her strength seemed to be coming back. She drank an Ensure and ate a little yogurt, and I stayed the night with her and convinced Natalie to go home and get some rest. She had a few personal days left that she was saving, so she showed up the next morning. Anna was able to sit up in the chair, but wanted to get back in bed after sitting up for about thirty minutes. She recognized us and wasn't nearly as confused, and we thought she had leaped over another tall hurdle.

Her hospitalist, Dr. Besh, from the cancer center came in, and it was great to see him. He was such a cool guy who had stayed on top of what was happening with Anna and oversaw her care on other visits. Anna perked up and answered his questions just as if she were perfectly well. He said he wanted her to get her strength back so she could begin a new chemo they had chosen for her, and we were flabbergasted with her response and again very optimistic. I followed him out in the hall and told him what Dr. No Tact had said, and Dr. Besh said that the liver numbers he mentioned didn't necessarily mean that her time was near and that chemo could still work. I texted Reid he was encouraged with his mom's turn around and Dr. Besh's assessment.

After lunch I went home, showered and took a nap and got my overnight bag. Natalie stayed until I returned, and we encouraged Anna to get up again, and she was able to drink another Ensure. She had eaten some solid food for lunch, but was still a little disoriented, though we were thinking she had once again beaten the odds. Dr. Besh ordered a brain MRI to see what might be causing the confusion and it revealed no cancer. Her liver specialist stopped by and said the cancer in the liver was most likely causing the mental problems, and I walked out in the hall and asked him if he thought the chemo would help. He didn't say yes, and I could tell by his nonverbal cues that he had serious doubts.

Tuesday night Anna was again extremely weak and confused and didn't eat much of her supper, but still gulped down the Ensure. By bedtime, she was less talkative and would call me Wallace, and she seemed agitated when I tried to help her to the bathroom. During the night she wasn't able to sit up in the bed, and Anna's dad was thinking it was time to bring her home on hospice. The next morning we called Reid and discussed this option with him. Had the doctors did all they could do? We agreed to wait until Dr. Besh came in the next morning and have a serious heart to heart talk with him.

Anna wasn't responding as well as she had the day before, and her abdominal swelling was increasing, and she couldn't lie on her stomach. We went out in the hall and Dr. Besh agreed, with tearful eyes, that it was time to take her home. We asked him if he thought if she had months or weeks because her vital signs were still perfectly normal. He said probably not months, but didn't think it would be in the next week or two, and we ordered hospice.

He suggested we do a procedure to drain the fluid from her abdomen before going home to make her more comfortable, but it was going to be the next morning before they could schedule it. They came to get her midmorning and she could still hold my hand and look up at me with her big brown loving eyes, nod her head, and squeeze my hand as I was accompanying her to get the procedure. The nurse said that she was able to drain hardly any fluid from her abdomen, which meant that it was all the tumor spreading rapidly.

We ordered an ambulance to take Anna back to the house, and Crossroads Hospice met us soon after arrival. We chose them because they had taken such good care of my mom the last six months of her life, and Anna had volunteered with them, sitting with their patients keeping them company. She mostly visited those who had few, if any, caring family members and were in nursing facilities. They brought oxygen, which Anna didn't need yet, and other meds, supplies, and a hospital bed the next morning. Anna was able to sit up in bed with our help and would guzzle down the Ensures. Her vital signs were all normal and the hospice nurse also thought her passing wasn't imminent.

I could tell she was happy to be back in her own bed, and she would look at me intently and follow me around the room. I kept telling her that Reid was on the way because his new boss had given him half a day off on Friday and told him to go see his mom. Reid got on speaker phone and told her how much he loved her and mentioned things that she had done for him, and her face brightened up. It had been a tough week for him wanting to be with his mom and fearing he would lose his job if he left. I told him that night that I honestly thought she would be around for a while longer.

Anna seemed comfortable and slept all night, but she didn't want to drink any Ensure or water when she woke up. When we tried to sit her up in the bed, she fussed and acted like it was hurting her, and when the hospice nurse arrived her blood pressure was no longer stable. It was dropping, and the nurse told us it was time to call the family, and we were surprised and got on the phone. Reid was preparing to leave Atlanta as planned, and Anna's brother Wallace and sister-in-law Sandra headed towards Memphis from Selmer. Her other brother, Ben, had come in from Oakland the night before on spring break and was staying with us. Anna's dad had become recently engaged and said he was on the way with his new fiancé, who Ben had not met.

I was hoping Reid would make it in time to see his mom, and his girlfriend, Madison, was coming with him, and I knew she would have a calming effect on him. Everyone arrived within a couple of hours except for Reid. Anna was looking around the room but seemed not to recognize any of us, and we gathered around the bed and spoke of the good times and how much she meant to us and prayed for God's grace and peace to fall on all of us.

The hospice nurse looked at the bottom of her feet, and they were suddenly turning blue, and she told us to immediately get everyone into the room because she could be gone at any minute. I called Reid and told him to pull over, and we got him on speaker phone and he spoke to Anna. She moved slightly, and I believed she heard him, and within a few minutes the angels came and took her home. Her last breaths were so very peaceful, unlike many I had been with during those moments, and I called Reid and told him to take his time.

Natalie finally broke down and let it all pour out, as did Anna's dad and myself. Anna had planned to donate her body to UT, and when I called them to let them know that it was time, they checked her records and saw the hip c from years ago and refused to come get her. I didn't know what to do but Google funeral homes and found one that was there within the next two hours. As they carried her out, Natalie, Joe, Wallace, Sandra, and I locked arms and sang "Will the Circle Be Unbroken" at the very top of our lungs. The circle was unbroken and there is not a doubt in any of our minds where she is. The circle was made complete in our eyes and in the eyes of God, and he had brought good out of this tragedy and restored us to Himself.

Reid arrived about an hour later, and we all broke down again with him and Madison. It was a tough, tough time, and I told them that one thing that can bring comfort is knowing they all did what they could for Anna, and they should have no regrets. I discovered from years in the homecare business, that is not always the case with family.

One of Anna's friends delivered meals sufficient to feed an army. It was very sad not being able to sleep by Anna's side that night and terribly hard waking up without her, but she wouldn't have to take all those pills and chemo treatments and wake up hurting during the night, as she had for the past nine months. Natalie, Reid, and Madison spent the night so we could be together the next morning. First thing, there was a knock on the door, and it was friends of Natalie's with Chick-fil-A biscuits and coffee. Natalie and Anna had ministered to their family after a tragic accident involving their niece.

Over the weekend, we had some very special time together with a few other close friends coming by to just be there for us. I couldn't help but weep as Reid drove off to head back home, and I cried more during those days than I had since I was a child. I had never really grieved a death, or any other loss, like that before. We decided to wait two weeks to have a memorial service for Anna.

Natalie was feeling like she could go back to work by the time Reid headed home, and her and Joe stopped by every night for the next week to check on me. Not only was Natalie concerned for her mom, but she also worried about my heart condition and other old man ailments, and she continues to touch base with me every day. Reid received timely news that his company had bought the packaging division of International Paper, which is based in Memphis. His boss allowed him to come back and work here the following week, with Thursday and Friday off.

Natalie had ideas for the memorial service, and we started making plans. The pastor of the church we were attending when we were very involved on the foreign mission field (including the former Soviet Union) agreed wholeheartedly to officiate the service and deliver the message, and Anna's brother, Ben, would lead the music. Working on the service was good therapy for us, finding old family photos and processing memories. Reid arrived the following week and began to create a slideshow with pictures and background music, and we put together a brief list of Anna's accolades and a program.

A few days before the service, Natalie and Joe approached me with Natalie somehow smiling and crying simultaneously and Joe grinning from ear to ear. Natalie was trying to say something and Joe told her, "Please tell your dad!"

Natalie said, "I just found out that I am pregnant!" What wonderful, timely news that was that almost left me speechless. The child would have been conceived before Anna passed away, and it was such a positive ray of hope and another sign that God was all over our circumstances. It was so bittersweet for Natalie because she had so wanted for Anna to be able to spend time with her first grandchild. Actually, Anna had become a grandmother before she died because the baby was growing in Natalie's womb. God is so amazing and kind to show up with this gift at such a perfect time.

We experienced an awesome celebration of Anna's life on Saturday. We had no clue how many would come, and then we found the fellowship hall at The Orchard Church packed with at least two hundred. People stood and shared stories about Anna and how she had blessed them, and Pastor Duke gave a fresh perspective of Anna's new home in heaven, which was so encouraging. We went back to the house with family and friends and had another celebration of Anna's life by setting off chalk multicolored bombs and everyone tossing different colors of powder up in the air, blanketing everyone that participated.

The next few weeks were especially rough, and it was hard to believe that she had gone on. Anna had planned the Colorado vacation for our family, and it was coming up about six weeks after the service. We knew that Anna would want us to go, and it would be a time to spend with immediate family preparing for a new beginning without her, and a time to celebrate my first grandchild which was on the way. We went and had a super relaxed time, and we each wore T-shirts proclaiming soon to be granddad, uncle, mom and dad. The coming child was there in Anna's place! Our comfort is the Blessed Hope and we will soon be together for all of eternity. The word for hope in the Bible means a fact that hasn't happened yet.

CONCLUSION

>‡X‡<

*T*his has been a story about what happens when we lose focus on the main thing. We face an enemy who is out to destroy families, and his attack was full of lies that promised a very bright future with our purest hopes and dreams set out before us. We were slowly following his advice, and how did we begin to drift? First, we joined hands with someone who had a world view that didn't line up with ours, and we missed early cues that should have been red flags. We decided to form a company with him without doing due diligence, and we paid him without him having any legal responsibilities and with zero financial investment. We didn't bathe the idea of working with him in prayer and proceeded full speed ahead, pedal to the metal. A friend told me not too long ago that when you drive like that, you are bound to run off in a ditch.

This appeared to us to be the right path, and we quickly zeroed in on business opportunities without finding out if there was a need. There wasn't a money making demand for anything that we tried, and when we asked potential customers in the Soviet Union what they needed, they would always respond by asking us what we had to offer, which sent us down countless rabbit holes. Another of the early signs we missed were the vodka toast that we thought were required to assimilate into their culture, which was a way of life for many of them. I had sworn off hard liquor many years ago and Anna hardly ever drank it. We had drunk beer or wine in recent years but never daily or even weekly. Even though I hated the taste of vodka, I found myself enjoying the buzz after more than a couple shots, and so did Anna. I really believe that gradually brought us back into a partying lifestyle, and it was a distraction from our calling.

Anna and I became less and less involved in church ministry and attendance, believing we were fulfilling God's purpose being away from home for extended periods as missionaries. Beyond a shadow of a doubt, we had been called into missions, and before this venture we could see the fruit of what we were doing in the lives of those we were reaching out to. Almost similar to ministering to street people, most of the folks in the former Soviet Union had extremely hard shells, and we weren't trained and equipped for that type of ministry.

Our relationship suffered from us being apart so much, with me being overwhelmed in a high stress business overseas, dealing with what turned out to be some very shady characters who didn't have my best interests at heart. I was informed later that I should have been concerned for my safety. Anna was working closely with Armad every single day, all day. That is something we should have recognized having counseled many couples, knowing that it can be unwise getting too close to coworkers of the opposite sex and depending on them for primary emotional support. If you sense that happening, you take a step back, and this didn't even occur to me. I take the blame for not realizing how I was neglecting to meet Anna's needs. We were both being caught up in different pursuits, mine being international business and hers getting deeply involved in the Russian culture and way of life.

Thank God he got my attention by bringing the FBI into the picture and putting the brakes on our activities with Russia. Anna didn't have this grateful perspective concerning their involvement, to say the least, because it was a threat to the most fulfilling work of her life. Instead of praying and working through this nightmare, we went our separate ways. Even a year afterwards, I didn't pray for our relationship, and God had to shake my world once again, and he knows how to do that, which is usually with my wallet. All of the money I had made was gone, and I was desperate and realized that God was the only one who could rescue me.

It was then that it suddenly dawned on me how far I had strayed, and I began crying out to Him. I soon remembered that God had put Anna and I together in the beginning, with lifelong vows, and I needed to pray for us to come back to Him, and then together as husband and wife. He used the strangest and most terrible circumstances to accomplish this by placing us together in a situation where neither of us had a choice. She needed me, and I needed her when no other person on earth could help either of us.

The scripture is true that ALL things work together for good for those that love God. He doesn't let us go and will pursue us to the ends of the earth. I know that there are times when divorce is absolutely necessary. I truly believe that our marriage wasn't over, and we could have worked through the ordeal, but we both stopped keeping the main thing the main thing.

God was with us every day through the cancer, and Anna knew it too. He gave both of us a second chance to come back together and to Him before He took her home. I am far from perfect and don't even consider myself religious, but I know I can't run away from Him outside of His love no matter what I do. I hope our journey that I have shared will encourage you and help you know that He is the God of second chances, even when we screw up royally like I did (and still do).

ABOUT THE AUTHOR

Mike describes himself as an old south Memphis ballplayer. He is an entrepreneur and has been self-employed for thirty-five years while spending time as a pastor and missionary. He loves people and launched a senior homecare franchise that grew into a multimillion-dollar business with ninety employees assisting over a thousand families. His main goal through the years has been to put his family first and hopefully make just a little time for golf. He is an excellent storyteller and his writing style combines a unique sense of humor with total honesty and transparency.

CPSIA information can be obtained
at www.ICGtesting.com
Printed in the USA
LVHW051124080920
665300LV00003B/409